UPMINSTER
In Living Memory

Edited by
Tony Benton

SWAN BOOKS, UPMINSTER

Published and distributed by:
Swan Books,
27 Corbets Tey Road,
Upminster,
Essex
RM14 2AR

First published October 2000

© Tony Benton and the authors, October 2000

ISBN 0 9503151 4 1

Printed and bound in Great Britain by
Lavenham Press Ltd.,
Water Street,
Lavenham,
Sudbury
Suffolk
CO10 9RN

CONTENTS

Editor's Introduction - Tony Benton 5

Happy memories of New Place - Muriel Sharp......................................7

An Upminster life - Hilda Halestrap 21

Upminster connections - Brian Moore..37

Hacton in the 1920s- Peter Hills 51

Upminster's Bonanza - June Muncey 65

Tadlows and other memories - Joan Hills 75

Open all hours: Bassett's tobacconists and confectioners - Peter Bassett............93

Upminster schooldays - Betty Heath 101

Index 115

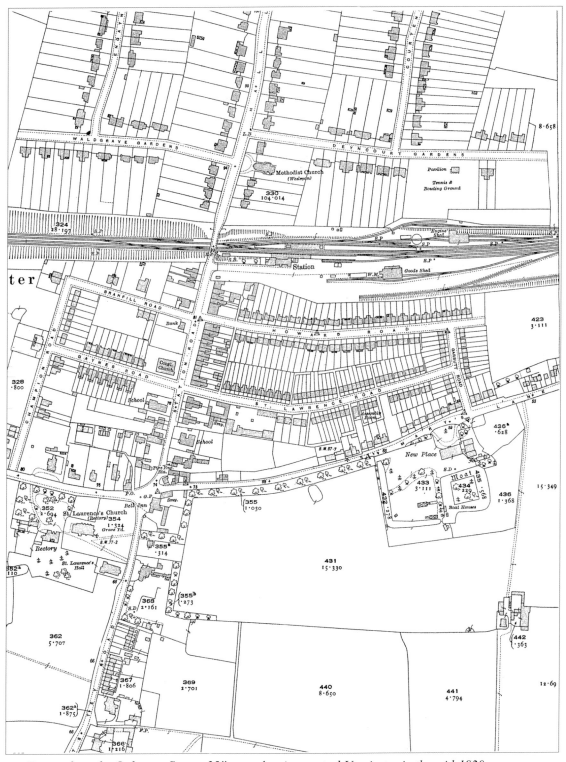

Extract from the Ordnance Survey 25" map showing central Upminster in the mid-1920s

Editor's Introduction

Tony Benton

Upminster - in living memory records the oral histories and reminiscences of eight authors, born between 1905 and 1933, who grew up or lived in Upminster in those now distant decades, sixty or more years ago. For all of them their earliest Upminster memories are those of childhood and most of these memories take us through to the period between the wars, when many had reached or were maturing into adulthood.

It is not surprising that a perspective of childhood comes through strongly, as the authors describe once again through a child's eyes a lost world where they and other children could wander far and wide through traffic-free lanes and play adventurously in the natural features of the countryside, such as water-filled gravel pits — features that today would be condemned as dangerous, to be avoided by children at all costs. The lost world of adults of an earlier, more formal, generation is also often glimpsed through children's eyes, and the even more distant past of the late Victorian era is accessed through stories handed down or heard years before, sometimes by inexperienced ears and which are now perhaps recalled for the first time in years.

We see from these personal narratives, however, that this seemingly idyllic freedom of a golden childhood was played out in a world where children's actions were forced to fit within strict boundaries of what was, or more typically wasn't, allowed by the norms set by Victorian or Edwardian adult society. A world where aunts and uncles paid scant attention to children, who as a result were left with often negative memories or an active dislike of their elder kinsfolk. In a few cases an affectionate memory shines through of those family friends or relations who defied the conventions of the times to turn a kindly blind eye to childish pranks or misdemeanours.

We also recall a world where personal or family tragedies were ever present, where young lives were too frequently touched by the loss or illness of a parent, brother or sister, or where families struggled to survive in changed circumstances or faced upheaval due to the uncertain economic times and loss of a job or business. There was also the impact of two world wars, which brought further losses of family or friends, and accelerated social changes.

The earliest period of these living memories takes us before the First World War when the development of the Upminster Garden Suburb was in its infancy and these memories continue through the period of rapid development and expansion which saw Upminster develop into a suburban town on the London fringes. Yet these narratives give little evidence that their authors have lived through these changes and it is only now, as they reflect on the nature of the world they have lost, that the scale of these changes comes into focus, through glimpses of what little has survived.

There may well be many other older current or former Upminster folk who feel that they have stories as equally as interesting as those that follow. The writers have been introduced to or made known to me in various ways over the last few years. In a few cases, finding out a little about their background, I have approached them "out of the blue" with an invitation to contribute a chapter and they have responded positively, if with a little trepidation. They are probably not a cross-section of old Upminster society, being biased towards the middle classes, as the various references to private education show, and the working population of Upminster appear more often as servants or employees than as key players in these stories.

There has been no standard approach to how chapters have been developed. Some chapters have been written up by me from notes of interviews and added to over several meetings with the authors' active involvement. Other chapters were written initially from correspondence from the author and expanded either after interviews or further letters. Some chapters have been written almost wholly by the authors, with only minor editing by me. In some cases other material provided by the authors has been woven into the text where relevant.

I hope that by presenting these personal histories I have preserved some of those things about Upminster that may not have been recorded in this way before. Perhaps by opening this window on the past it gives those of us of a later generation some insight into the world of our parents and grandparents and, by understanding this better, helps us understand our modern world better still.

Upminster, August 2000

Happy Memories of New Place

Muriel Sharp

My parents Herbert Sharp and Maud Wilson were married in St Laurence Church Upminster on 1 July 1903. My father, known as Bertie, who was then aged 32 and living in Acton, was a stockjobber on the London Stock Exchange. My mother Florence Maud (but known only as Maud), was aged 26, the eldest daughter of John and Emily Wilson of New Place, Upminster, who both originated in the Highlands of Scotland. They are buried in the Upminster parish churchyard to the right of the entrance, in a grave entirely covered with Scotch granite stone. I always thought of grandmother Wilson as being a very old lady but she was only 76 when she died in 1924. Their youngest son Roy and his wife Bobbie are buried in the same grave.

My parents' first home was Burnside, Hornchurch Road, a four bed-roomed semi-detached house which still survives almost opposite to Upminster Bridge railway station. At that time there were no other buildings towards Upminster until the Bridge House Inn and the River Ingrebourne, which marked the boundary with Upminster.

Muriel and John Sharp outside Malvern, Hall Lane c.1911

I was born on New Year's Eve 1908 at Burnside, the third of their offspring to be born there, the others being my older brother John, born in April 1904, and a sister Margaret, who died as a baby. I was named Muriel Maud Sharp and I was baptised in Hornchurch's St Andrew's Church on 3 February 1909. I have no memories of my first home in Hornchurch as, when I was less than two years old and before my younger sister Eileen Janet was born in June 1910, we moved to a new detached house in Hall Lane which my father called Malvern after his old school. This was located just past the junction with Waldegrave Gardens, next to Miss Brown's school, known as Upminster High School. My very first memory is of being pushed in the pram with Eileen by a nursemaid over Upminster Bridge when a wheel came off the pram. I was lifted out and had to walk home, presumably to Malvern, holding onto the pram. I was not happy!

I spent much of my first 14 years in Upminster and often visited after that—right up to the Second World War when I was sent abroad. I remember so well all the traders in Station Road. Jupp the butcher's, next door to the boys' school, Frizzell the baker, Searsons the shoe shop, Wright the newsagent and the Crumpled Horn Dairy. One shopping trip I can vividly recall was a visit with my mother to Mr Gooderham's grocers store on the corner of Howard Road. Somehow I became separated from her and screamed and screamed in distress but all the time we were both still in Mr Gooderham's shop, which was by no means large.

In my day the two Miss Battsons served in the diary on the corner of St Lawrence Road. I remember the Bon Marché so well — it had low shelves with small toys that my sister and I stood and gazed at. I can also recall the two shops round the corner from Aggiss the coach builders — later Aggiss' Chestnuts Garage. These faced the churchyard, each with a step up to them. One was an excellent haberdasher (Miss Collis) but I can't remember who owned the other one.

Looking east towards Cosy Corner, St Mary's Lane, Eldred's Forge and the Bell Inn.

I remember the grocers on Upminster Hill opposite Hill House School, which was the only shop there. I have a memory of articles for sale outside and I know I went into it once or twice with either grandmother or her housekeeper Eliza (of whom see later). I also recall visiting Upminster Mill, probably with Eliza, I think to buy flour. We saw Mr Abraham the miller, who wore a cap, and whose clothes were covered in the fine dust of the flour. The Cosy Corner was very popular locally but it was not the "done thing" for young ladies such as us to go there. How longingly we children would admire those customers sitting on the seats outside eating and drinking, so obviously enjoying that which we were so snobbily denied!

During the First World War my father was a special constable whose job was to place either a green or red lamp in a small hole in a hut built the Hall Lane side of the railway bridge to indicate "Air raid" or "All clear". I saw the Zeppelin which was brought down by Lt Leefe Robinson at Cuffley in September 1916. My mother woke me up from sleep to see it blazing in the night sky and I am sure that she recognised the significance of this as an historical event.

My parents had many good friends in the area. Dr Bletsoe whose surgery was on the corner of Branfill Road, of course, was one (although our family doctor was Sam Wright from Romford). Others include the George Eves of Hoppey Hall, on the right hand side of Corbets Tey Road, who had a son born the same week as I was, the Plattens of Harwood Hall and their daughter Mrs Norton, Mr Thompson of Cranham, a business associate of my father's, and Mr W G Key, a Director of W P Griggs & Co., who had developed the Upminster Garden Suburb, who lived near us in Hall Lane. The Hollicks were other great family friends in my mother's circle, as were the Attenboroughs, who lived in a house on the left-hand side of the Hornchurch Road, near Miss Rilley's Hill House School. Another name I remember were the Brookfields, who I believe must have been Dr Storrs

Deyncourt Gardens in the 1920s

Brookfield who lived at Hill Place. The Joslins — Walter Joslin of Hunts Farm in Corbets Tey Road and his brother Henry of Gaynes Manor — were friends of my grandparents.

I went to Miss Smith's kindergarten school in Ashburnham Gardens. I remember that I had a friend there named Kathy Bonsall who lived in a house on Hall Lane between Waldegrave Gardens and the bridge, which had (I think) a sloping garden at the front. My greatest treat was for grandfather to fetch me from school with his horse and carriage with Scarff, the coachman, on the box and take me back to New Place. Grandfather had two carriages, a Victoria and a Landau and two horses, Duchess and Jack. Later, when I was about eleven and I went to stay with two elderly aunts at Highgate (my grandmother's spinster sisters), I attended a day school there called Morven School. After that I was a boarder at Southwood Hall, Muswell Hill/Archway, North London, until, when I was 16, I attended Nursery Training School at Wellgarth Road, London NW11.

After some years at Malvern, Hall Lane my parents later moved to 11 Deyncourt Gardens nearby in Upminster. One day, when mother was not well, father took my sister and I to the field at the end of Deyncourt Gardens and told us to run across the fields to New Place and tell Eliza the housekeeper that mother was poorly. But a few years later it was father who was unwell. He was taken ill at work and admitted to St Thomas' Hospital, London where he died of cancer of the liver a week later on 24 October 1920, aged 49. I remember that Eileen and I had to wear black mourning dresses made by grandmother. They were long and ugly and we absolutely hated them. We were embarrassed at school — we felt "different"! At the end of the eight-week mourning period grandmother told us that we needn't wear them any more. We were so excited that we threw them out of the bathroom window into the garden below. Needless to say, Eliza sent us to pick them up. We also had to wear black ribbon on our panama school hats instead of the usual school colour: these ribbons also went out of the window as well.

Poor mother was devastated by father's death: three children, very little money and no bread-winner. With no widow's pension, child benefit or NHS in those days it is understandable that she suffered a bout of deep depression. I think that at that time there must have been a family conference and it was decided that our home at 11 Deyncourt Gardens must be given up and that our grandparents would pay for mine and Eileen's education, while Uncle Percy, my father's brother, would become John's guardian. Mother, when better, would try to find a job — unheard of for a married woman in those days. My brother John at that time was a boarder at Alleyn Court School, Westcliff-on-Sea where he wore a pink cap embroidered in white with "A.C." Later, he went on to Merchant Taylor's School and qualified to join the Merchant Navy as Wireless Officer. I think that John suffered from this bereavement much more than we girls did. He was 15 when father died and it was a terrible upheaval for him to go away to live with Uncle Percy in Hampstead, London.

Mother was soon better and she managed to get a job as housekeeper in a nurses' home attached to a hospital. She did well and was happy there as she said herself "I am always busy". Later, she was appointed as Sewing Matron at the Orthopaedic Hospital at Stanmore. She was a very good needlewoman and with two girls under her supervision made all the nurses' uniforms. When mother joined the staff at the hospital she rented a flat in Stanmore where Eileen stayed in school holidays and I was able to visit. When I was at Southwood Hall Eileen went to the Welsh Girls' School at Ashford, Middlesex as mother wanted her to be near where she worked. How mother managed to get Eileen in there I don't know as we have no Welsh blood! Eileen did well and then went to Pitman's Secretarial College and became a secretary book-keeper later marrying Charles Phillips-Smith and had two children, my niece and nephew Elisabeth and Edward. They are now my only relatives and they are both very dear to me, as I know I am to them. They are both so good to me and visit me often. I go to stay periodically with Elisabeth, who has a delightful bungalow at King's Sutton, near Banbury where Edward too has a bungalow. He is a chaplain of a prep school and Elisabeth is a nurse.

During World War Two mother looked after eight boys, evacuees from London, in a country house in Potten End, Hertfordshire, afterwards retiring to a little cottage in the same village. I was with her when she died on her 96th birthday on 6 December 1973 in Queensway House, a nursing home in Hemel Hempstead.

My grandfather John Wilson was born in 1846, the son of Robert Wilson, a Glasgow merchant, and he was educated at Dollar Academy, Clackmannanshire. He trained for five years as a mechanical engineer in the locomotive shops and Engine Works of the Great Western Railway at Worcester and, after serving his articles as a mechanical engineer, he came to London and was articled as a civil engineer to Mr Edward Wilson, consulting and contracting engineer for Great Western, Great Eastern and other railways. He became a Member of both the Institutions of Mechanical and Civil Engineers (M.I.C.E and M.I.M.E). Among the many extensive works he was engaged on were the Great Eastern's Metropolitan extension and the Liverpool Street Station, as well as railway extensions in Norfolk and further afield. On Mr Edward Wilson's death in 1877 grandfather became a partner in the firm of Messrs Edward Wilson and Company, and during this time the extensive quay and warehouses at Parkeston in Essex were completed. He remained with the company as partner until 1883 when he was appointed Engineer-in-Chief to the Great Eastern Railway. In 1907 it was said that he held the record as the longest serving Railway-Engineer-in-Chief.

Grandfather married Emily, daughter of Mr Swarbrick, General Manager of Great Eastern Railway and they had eight children, of whom seven, four boys and three girls, survived. The boys were: Edward, who became Chief Engineer of the Metropolitan Railway but later sadly committed suicide; Jack and Herbert, who were both killed in World War I, Herbert at Gallipoli; and Robert ("Roy"). The girls were: Maud, my mother; Margaret (Aunt Maggie); and Eleanor (Aunt Nell).

My grandfather was a great fly fisher who spent many days pursuing his hobby on the

Front entrance to New Place with members of the Wilson family on the steps

John Wilson with his granddaughters Muriel and Janet at New Place, c. 1913

banks of the River Wye. I have a copy of a paper of his entitled "Fishing, angling and anecdotes" which was read before the members of the Retired Railway Officers' Society on 10 January 1922. In this he describes the various locales, habits, lifestyles and features of Brown Trout, Sea Trout, Salmon and Grayling, which he says were the fish he had been in the habit of angling for. It appears that he was fondest of the latter, which he described as "a most delicate and delicious dish" that he much preferred to Salmon or Trout when cooked to his own "receipt".

Grandfather had a bungalow at Battlesbridge in Essex whose garden, as a railway man, led by a gate to the railway platform. Eileen and I often stayed there with him with Eliza and we picked bunches of flowers and went to the platform to give them to the engine drivers.

How well I remember my grandparents' grand home of New Place! The house was approached from Cranham Road (later renamed St Mary's Lane) by two huge iron gates that were always open, one to go in and one to go out. The front garden was semi-circular with grass in the middle of a wide drive and an enormous cedar of Lebanon tree in the centre. I was told that this tree, one of the landmarks which typically denoted Esdaile's former Upminster properties, was the second largest such tree in England. The very wide front door, which had a noisy bell-pull, was approached by five white stone steps to a porch, over which was a bow window. The top half of the front door was coloured glass, which looked like the coloured circles of the bottom of wine glasses; one couldn't see through it.

I can still remember the interior of New Place as if I had visited it just yesterday. The front door led to a very big hall, which had on the wall a large glass case, containing an enormous fish (dead!), possibly one that grandfather had caught. Also in the hall were two

Inside New Place - The Drawing Room

stags' heads with antlers, and a fox's mask. Off the hall was a large cloakroom which we children were not allowed to use — it was grandfather's domain. He kept a spare pair of false teeth in a glass of water on the side of the washbasin and every day, so as to use the right pair of dentures, he enquired of Eliza "What was he eating for lunch?"! Next in the hall were the very elegant front stairs with thick patterned carpet, brass stair rods and wrought iron banisters. Again, as children, we were not allowed to use these front stairs. Half way up, where the stairs turned, was a grandfather clock. Grandmother had a little black dog called a Toy Pomeranian, named Jim Crow. I can, even now, visualize grandmother coming down these lovely stairs with the little dog at her heels.

Next, was the green baize door that led through a passage to the kitchen. There was a very long dresser, on which were plates, vegetable dishes and soup tureens, a very big kitchen range, a table in the middle for preparing meals on and, under the window, another table where Eliza and the staff had their meals. Eileen and I always had tea in the kitchen: we loved this as we were allowed to eat as much bread and golden syrup (no butter) as we wanted. There was always a huge laundry hamper in the corner of the kitchen: the household laundry was sent to an outside laundry and was collected and delivered each week. Through the kitchen was a door leading to stone steps down to the larder and, out of that, steps down to the cellar, which was very cold. Opposite the kitchen door was the "still room", with cupboards from floor to ceiling, where all the preserves such as jam and marmalade were kept. Grandfather had something to do with a new railway line to Tiptree in Essex and at Christmas he was always sent a complimentary case of Tiptree jam. Further down the passage was the back door, with steps down to the stable yard. Just before the back door were the linoleum-covered back stairs which led to the billiard room and second floor.

The next door off the hall after the green baize passage door was the dining room, with dining table and chairs, two sideboards and a small table where grandfather always sat to have his 6.00 p.m. "high tea". Why he never sat at the dining table for that meal I don't know, as he always sat there for his midday meal. On the other side of the hall was the ante room that led to the drawing room and then the library. The drawing room, which I remember as almost completely filled with all its fussy Victorian and Edwardian furniture, was originally the ballroom of the house built by Sir James Esdaile. It had an Adam fireplace and in each corner of the ceiling was a cornice of Aesop's fable of the fox and the grapes. The drawing room furniture that I remember was a Broadwood grand piano, a Louis XIV chaise de longue, a spinning wheel, and two upright armchairs that grandmother told me had been made specially for her by Mr Gillow of Waring & Gillow of London. She had met him on a ship's cruise where he had supplied the comfortable armchairs, so she ordered them. Also in the drawing room was a bow-fronted cabinet of very dark wood with a mirror. This belonged to my Aunt Maggie who used it as a music cabinet. She gave it to me when she went to live in Vancouver in Canada. I have that in my home today and I use it daily for files and books.

My grandparents always sat in the library, which was lined with book-filled bookcases. The drawing room was only used at high days and holidays, such as Christmas and parties. Grandmother liked us to play card games and board games with her and, in those days before television, she taught me to play bridge, whist, chess, draughts and other games. Grandmother did the most exquisite cotton crochet work. She made beautiful tablecloths, tray cloths and other pieces, which I have now passed to my niece Elisabeth, who uses them. A sideboard cloth edged with wide crochet lace, made for my mother's wedding and marked with marking ink with her name and dated 1903, is now on the credence table in the parish church in Potten End where I worship.

Halfway up the back stairs was a passage that led to the billiard room and workshop. At the beginning of the passage was a lavatory which housed a toilet pan, set in a long mahogany surround, and the handle to flush was a pull up affair, also set in the mahogany.

Next were two steps down to the billiard room, which had big low lights over the billiard table, a rack for the billiard cues, and a device for scoring. Eileen and I were allowed to play with the cues and balls but we weren't much good. Out of the billiard room was grandfather's workshop. His great hobby was carpentry. During the First War he made splints and other accessories for the war wounded and the local hospitals relied on him to keep them supplied.

At the top of the back stairs was a sewing room, then Eliza's room and the room where we slept, which was always called Uncle Roy's room. Next door to our room was a locked communicating room which was grandfather's room; there was another communicating door to grandmother's room, unlocked and always open. Grandfather liked to have a bowl of fresh stewed fruit (no tins in those days) put by his bed at night — I remember being woken up at night hearing the clink of the spoon against the bowl when grandfather was eating.

Florence Maud Sharp née Wilson and gardeners at New Place

The upstairs landing was beautifully carpeted with a big bow window with window seats that was over the front porch. Off this landing was the morning room, which doubled up as a nursery. On the mantelpiece was a black marble pendulum clock with wind-up key and I now have that very clock here in my home. At least 90 years old, and maybe more, it keeps perfect time and gives me much pleasure. Also off the landing was a big spare bedroom, another door into grandmother's room and a bathroom. The staff bedrooms were up another flight of stairs: I only once went up there, I think that there were four rooms, maybe a sitting room too.

Attached to the house at the side of the kitchen was a conservatory and a fishing room where fishing rods and tackle were kept. Two fishing rods were put aside for we children to use. Eileen and I spent hours fishing in the moat for roach and carp. We rolled bread into tiny balls for bait. Grandfather had taught us how to take the hook from the fish's mouth and to throw the fish back into the water. The conservatory was bow shaped and had several slatted shelves running the length of it but I don't think it was used much. We had to go through it to the fishing room but I can't remember flowers or plants in there.

As befitted a house of this kind my grandparents employed a number of staff. Mr Scarff

Rear view of New Place

the coachman lived in a cottage behind the stables. Once a week grandmother went shopping to Romford and I would go with her in the carriage. I remember that before one such trip, while waiting for grandmother to come out of the house, I engaged in conversation with the coachman. "Scarff", I enquired, "how do the horses know where to stop when we get to Romford?" "Why, don't you know miss?", Scarff replied with a twinkle in his eye, "Haven't you noticed that after your grandmother has got into the carriage and I have put the rug over her knee, I whisper to the horse 'Next stop Sainsbury's and then Boots'." For several years I believed what the coachman had said and it was quite a blow to me when I found out the truth!

The gardener at New Place was Mr Claxson, who had nine or ten children, one of whom, Bessie, used to suffer from fits. My grandfather always wore a buttonhole: Mr Claxson cut a bloom from the garden and placed it beside grandfather's place at the breakfast table in a metal, probably silver, water-filled container which grandfather was able to place in the button hole of his jacket.

My grandparents employed a cook and three maids, Annie, Daisy and Eliza. I remember when I was very young I watched Daisy ironing grandmother's handkerchiefs, all of which had her initial "E" in the corner. I could never understand how Daisy always managed to fold the hankies so as to get the initial on the outside of the folded hankie! Now I wonder why I wondered!

The latter maid, Eliza Anne Cook, was little older than my mother. Born nearby at Cranham, she had gone to work for grandmother as a 13-year-old live-in maid and stayed

16

on for many years until grandma's death. She was a wonderful housekeeper to my grandparents, and she would wear a great big white apron and a high white cap, which we called a crown. She was a lovely person, if a little eccentric. One of her eccentricities concerned spectacles: if someone wearing a pair of glasses came into the house it was her practice to remove them and to give them a polish before returning them to the often surprised visitor. Another foible concerned umbrellas: she would always unfurl any umbrella she came across and roll it back up tightly in much neater fashion than she had found it. We were always very happy at New Place because Eliza loved us so much. When we wanted to do anything special, we always asked Eliza to approach grandmother, who we were a little bit afraid of, although I don't know why.

After we moved away I stayed in touch with Eliza and in later years when we returned to visit Upminster I would go to see her in the house named Meadway that she shared in Ingrebourne Gardens. She died in 1942 when I was away in Canada and she is buried in Cranham churchyard. I became a "nanny" looking after many babies and children; Eliza was a great example to me and I tried so hard to be like her. I think I succeeded.

I have vivid memories of the almost ritual-like life at New Place. On Fridays, dead on 5.00 p.m., the front door bell would ring and Eliza would usher in first the coachman and then the gardener and garden boy to collect their wages from grandmother. Why my grandmother paid them and not my grandfather I don't know. Also on Fridays, at a certain time in the morning, Eliza would come to the library and escort grandmother to the kitchen. There cook put everything ready for grandmother to make a batch of pastry — pastry board and rolling-pin, flour, fat etc. I was allowed to watch and, when the pastry was made, I was given a small ball of dough which I shaped into a mouse, with sultanas for its eyes. This was cooked with the other pastry and it always tasted good! I never remember grandmother going to the kitchen at any other time or for her to do any other cooking. Usually cook came to the library every morning for "orders". I don't know whether grandmother cooked on Friday because she didn't like cook's pastry or whether she wanted to have a hand in the domesticity of her own home.

At the far end of the hall was a door leading to the garden, down several metal steps with handrails either side. Looking from the garden door at the back of the house there was a very formal garden with shaped flowerbeds, the plants being changed at seasons of the year. There were two bushes of pampas grass and a big monkey-puzzle tree, beyond which was the moat with iron rails about waist high, and a larger island in the middle, where ducks and moor-hens nested. Looking out from the drawing-room windows was a very big lawn with shrubs on the left hand side - two huge rhododendron bushes at the top and a cedar tree which had a swing on one of its branches. These divided the lawn from the kitchen garden. On the right hand side was a path, edging a herbaceous border and a long brick wall, on which were espalier fruit trees. I can remember green-gages, peaches, plums, pears and figs. When the fruit was ripe we were allowed to pick up and eat any that had fallen — it's surprising how much "fell"!

We were not usually allowed in the kitchen garden at New Place except on summer evenings where we were permitted to go there when on our walk under Eliza's supervi-

The Clockhouse, the former stable block of New Place. This photo dates from the period when it was used as Upminster's library

sion. I remember that there were a number of fruit trees. One tree that I especially remember, as it was at the entrance to the garden, was a quarendon apple tree, small bright pink apples that tasted delicious. I've never been able to find that apple — I wish I could — to find out if it tasted as good now. There were also two vineries, one with black grapes and the other white, and on these walks I would often be allowed to pick a bunch. The kitchen garden paths were lined with very low box hedges and inside this hedge in springtime there were masses of daffodils, a lovely sight. At the far end of the kitchen garden was a woodshed. I loved to watch the gardener and boy sawing wood logs on a trestle with a double-handed saw. I was allowed to go there as there was another path to it, which did not run through the kitchen garden which we were usually forbidden to enter. (On reading through these notes I notice how often I have said "we were allowed (or not allowed)". I suppose this is discipline: anything out of the ordinary we were expected to ask permission for.)

From the lawn of New Place the shrubbery — it was called "The Walk" — ran for hundreds of yards through the New Place Estate grounds right behind the Bell Inn up to the gate opposite St Laurence's church. As children we loved this and we were allowed to go unaccompanied to watch the Mr Eldred, the blacksmith at work at his forge alongside the Bell Inn. On Sundays we were accompanied on our walks along the shrubbery on our way to church where I would sit in the back pew with Eliza. On these summer evening walks with Eliza we would also go to the paddock to feed the horses and we would sometimes hear the sound of the bells ringing from St Andrew's church, Hornchurch a couple of miles away across the valley. When I hear the chime of bells it still brings back memories of those magical Upminster childhood days over 80 years ago.

Postscript

In August 1998 my nephew Edward asked me if I would like to visit Upminster to have a "look around", if so he would be pleased to take me there. I jumped at the offer. On the 22nd he and Elisabeth came to fetch me. I had gathered a small bunch of flowers to place on my grandparents' grave and took a bag of bread-crusts to feed the ducks, if some were still there.

We entered Upminster along Hall Lane and I recognised the Hall at once, but not all the houses there — when I lived in Upminster Hall Lane was still a country lane. We found Deyncourt Gardens and Edward took a photo of No. 11, our former home. What a maze of houses led into it! I remember Deyncourt Gardens as being a short road with fields at the bottom.

We eventually found our way to St Mary's Lane but drove past two or three times before we found the entrance to Clockhouse Gardens. I was thrilled to see the dear old clock that I knew so well which in my day had chimed every hour. I was delighted to find the moat still there. I stood and fed the ducks in exactly the same place as I had done as a child.

I can't think why such a fuss was made to preserve Clockhouse, which used to be the stable block to New Place, when the main house itself was sold and demolished a few years after grandfather died in November 1922. I was sad to see New Place gone but delighted to see a young monkey-puzzle tree which had been planted in the same place as the old

Clockhouse Gardens, late 1940s

big one. From that I could get my bearings. The old railings round the moat were still there but almost sunk into the ground. We walked round the moat — the old big cedar tree with branches over the water had gone but we were treading the same old path. We walked round the back of the moat but what had been fields was now houses. Two more cedar trees had gone. The kitchen garden and lawn were now bowling greens and it is nice to know that the gardens haven't been entirely destroyed but put to another use.

We went down St Mary's Lane to the cross roads — I recognised the cross roads but not as such a busy place and I had never seen shops and traffic lights there before this. In my time there were two little cottages with orchards on the right hand side of the road occupied by Miss Warren and Mrs Bone. Eileen and I loved to talk to them when they came to the gates to greet us as we walked towards the village.

I visited my grandparents' grave and we all went to the church, which was larger than when I was there, I think another chapel has been built. It felt good to be back there again. Edward took photos, both inside and out.

I hardly recognised Upminster — so many shops etc. and the station now at the top of the road. In my time the station was down the road at the side and Eileen and I used to walk down there to meet our brother John from boarding school at holiday time. I know that all little villages such as Upminster was must grow in time but was amazed that it had grown into a London suburb. But for me the nucleus of Upminster was still there — the Clockhouse Gardens and the clock of which I now have a photograph, together with others, on a poster over my desk.

A lovely happy day, a real nostalgic one. Perhaps we'll do it again one day?

Potten End, Hertfordshire. April 2000

An Upminster Life

Hilda Halestrap

Upminster was not my first home but it has been my abode for the past 90 or so years, since my family moved to 23 St Lawrence Road in October 1908 when I was nearly three.

I was born at 62 Balvernie Grove, Southfields, in south-west London (now SW18) a few days before Christmas 1905. At that time my father Frederick Halestrap was a coachman to a lady (Mrs Swann) there but later decided to return to Essex to work for his brother Walter, who ran a decorators' business from North Street, Hornchurch, next to the premises of Frosts Motor Company. My mother Mary (she was born Amelia Mary Wilby but was known as Mary) had been in service as a parlourmaid in the same area of London that my father worked, so I assume that they met there. Like my father she too had originated in Essex, born in January 1870 at Great Horkesley, near Colchester, where her father Thomas Wilby was a gardener at the Rectory, living at the lodge at the Rectory gates. When my parents married at St Stephen's parish church, Twickenham in March 1902 they were both over 30 years old. My father, born in December 1870, was 31 and my mother,

Wedding of Frederick Halestrap and Amelia Mary Wilby, March 1902

11 months his senior, was aged 32. At that time my father was living at Disraeli Road, Putney and mother at Riverdale Gardens, Twickenham. After their wedding they set up home in a flat at Southfields, where my older brother Frederick (Fred) was born in July 1903, with my birth following there over two years later.

I was the middle of three children, with my older brother Fred and Ernest (Ernie), who was almost 9 years younger than me, born in October 1914 when mother was already 44 years old. When I was old enough to go to school this was only a short walk away down St Lawrence Road to the Infants' and Girls School, in the Old British School buildings almost opposite, while my brother went to the Boys' School on our side of the Broadway (now known as Station Road). When I was in the infants' a small boy, Ralph Woolf, who lived with his parents at the restaurant (Woolfs) on the corner of St Lawrence Road, used to come and call for me and we became good pals.

Hilda Halestrap (centre front row) Upminster Girls and Infants School, 1912

I remember that in the Girls' School Miss Berry was our headteacher with Miss Aggiss her assistant. In the Infants' Miss Pearce from Hornchurch was the headmistress, while another teacher was Miss Constance Eldred, whose family owned the forge alongside the Bell. The Headmaster at the Boys' School was Mr West - known by all as "Daddy" for reasons not known to me. On Empire Day we all went to the Boys' School opposite, where Mr Henry Joslin, from Gaynes Manor House, gave a short talk about the British Empire. All the girls wore in their buttonholes a small bunch of daisies, tied with red, white and blue ribbon. After Mr Joslin's speech we all sang a hymn and the national anthem, before we were then allowed the rest of the day off as a holiday.

My mother was always there for us when we needed her when we were young. It was a comforting feeling to know that she would be waiting for us at home with a drink and biscuit or piece of cake when we ran home after our day at the village school and that she would be waiting again when we came back home at tea time after playing out with our friends.

Sometimes after school we would buy our sweets in Abrahams shop close by. We would keep watch until we spotted that Florrie Abraham was serving, as she was known to be more generous than her mother. Sweets were served in little twists of newspaper: I don't know what they would say now about this but we never came to any harm. I also remember that we would take cans to Hunts Farm in Corbets Tey Road to collect milk, either skimmed or new. The dairy led through into stone-floored kitchen where Mrs Wakefield would serve us. We children used to crowd round the kitchen door waiting to be served and she would say "I'm not serving you until you stand back". She always said this phrase, and on occasions we would say it for her!

But in my younger days Upminster didn't seem to be a village where much ever happened. Perhaps that's why I can recall the excitement of the time in 1916 when during the First World War the first Zeppelin was shot down by Lt Robinson from Suttons Farm airfield in Hornchurch. My father was too old to be called up for the forces but many of the young men who died were well known to me, including two sons of the large Caldecourt family who lived near the boys' school. We had soldiers billeted at our house. Those I remember were a Mr Lovejoy and a Mr Cox, a farmer, both from the Bucks Regt., a Mr Waugh, a Scotsman, and a Mr Dickinson, who I remember was very popular at dances!

Silk Christmas card from W Huckle, RAMC

I think it must have been in the early months of the war in 1914 that along with fellow pupils at the Girls' School we knitted mittens for local men serving with the forces in France. I still have the woven silk greetings card received from W. Huckle, R.A.M.C (Royal Army Medical Corps) serving with the B.E.F. France which records the message "I send this card in grattitude (*sic*) of your splendid work and nice little letter which was very well written and the mits will be a great comfort to me this winter. Wishing you a happy Christmas." I think that this probably must have been Bill Huckle who, in later years, was caretaker of the church hall and cared for the churchyard.

When I was eleven I went on to Romford County High School for Girls, where Miss Frances Bardsley was the first head mistress - this school which still survives in Heath Park Road, Romford is now named after her. Miss Bardsley - or "Barge" as we all called her - was a good headmistress. She was a big woman who I remember always walked around wearing a flowing gown. Although I don't think we were afraid of her, we certainly respected her a great deal. After she retired I heard that one night someone had broken into her bedroom while she was there. Miss Bardsley sat up in bed and stared at the intruder, who turned on his heel and fled and I can't say we were surprised to hear his reaction!

Romford County High School in 1912, a few years before Hilda Halestrap's attended there

My five years at the County High School were very happy ones and I made many friends who I kept in touch with for years to come. In summer I would cycle to school but during the winter months I would take the train from Upminster to Romford with my friends, picking up others who got on at Emerson Park Halt on the way. From Romford Station we had a long walk down Victoria Road to the school. I was very keen on sport. Miss Cartwright was our teacher and I played hockey in winter and cricket and tennis in summer on our large sports ground adjoining the railway line. I also took great pleasure from drawing lessons under our Art teacher, Miss Nation.

But in 1922 when I was sixteen, it was time to move on and I left my happy school days behind to work for Smith and Ebbs, a firm of printers in Northumberland Alley, near Fenchurch Street. I joined them as a junior and I remained for 42 years. After the war, when the Managing Director and Secretary retired, the firm was reorganised and I became the Company Secretary.

Between the wars Upminster seemed so carefree as we pursued our own interests, many of which revolved around St Laurence Church. When we were small we attended Sunday School at the church under the Rev. Holden, with the boys arranged on one side and the girls the other. My brothers Fred and Ernie were both members of the choir and also acted as servers, while Fred went on to help out in many ways, sweeping the churchyard paths, doing odd jobs etc. He was also a stalwart of the 1st Upminster Scout Group from their formation in 1917 right through into the 1950s, starting as a boy scout and staying on to become Scoutmaster and Rover leader. Fred was also a member of the Upminster Volunteer Fire Brigade in the late 1920s. There was regular training for the brigade and it was also important for them to test to make sure that all the hoses they would use and the fire hydrants around the parish were in good working order for when they might be needed. The volunteers were called out by the ringing of a bell. If this happened during the night, as it sometimes did, Fred would leap out of bed and Dad would help him into his uniform while Ernie would open all the doors and gates to make sure his exit was unhindered. Most fires were stack fires and I particularly remember a bad fire up at Hall Lane

Upminster Fire Brigade, late 1920s. Fred Halestrap seated centre

near to Birds Lane, which it seemed all of Upminster went to watch.

I was a choir member for over 50 years, joining in 1922 and remaining until the early 1970s. In the 1920s the choir, under the guidance of the choirmaster Mr Gerald Sykes, was a large one and the members were from some of Upminster's leading business families, such as the Roomes, Gates, the estate agents, and the Keys of Upminster Estates. The

Rev. Holden with May Queens, May Festival 1927. Miss Coles is seated in the front row, holding the bouquet

Jupp family were also prominent members with, at one time, six of them taking part: old Mr Jupp the butcher; his son and daughter; his son's wife and two of their children. At Christmas members of the choir would go out carol singing and I remember that we went to Gaynes Manor where we sang in the hall for Mr Henry Joslin. When we had finished the butler would come up to us with a large tray bearing Mr Joslin's donation.

In 1913 the Rev. Hyla Henry Holden, our Rector from 1904 to his death in 1944, originated Upminster's May Festival, which was held one Saturday each May. Miss Coles, an Upminster resident who was the headmistress of Westbury School in Barking, arranged the festival from 1913 until 1937. The day would start with a service in St Laurence church and a procession would make its way across the junction at the Bell and into Station Road, up to the railway station. A band always led the procession. In the early years this was the Westbury Girls' School Orchestra, later it was the band of the Hornchurch Cottage Homes, and later still the Upminster St Laurence Scouts' band. The local people would come out to watch and put their coppers and loose change into the collecting tins proffered by the helpers. From the station the procession made its way back towards the church, assembling on the Rectory Lawn, where there would be dancing around the maypole and other festivities. The May Queen, usually aged about 15 or 16, was chosen from those girls attending Sunday school and quite a crowd of up to six young "maids of honour" supported her. It was very much a pageant and many helpers wore costumes to add colour to the occasion, including a "Prime Minister" wearing a powdered wig who would flourish a scroll before making his formal announcements and introductions to the assembled audience. The queen would be crowned by the Rector and presented with a bible. Later that day, the newly crowned queen would host a reception in the St Laurence Church Hall.

It was my privilege to be crowned as Upminster's Queen in May 1922 and at my reception my cousin Arthur, who had a good tenor voice, sang a couple of ballads. It was the custom for queens from previous years to come back to support the festivities each year. As a former queen who still lived in Upminster, I took part in this occasion annually up to the outbreak of war in 1939, after which the festival ceased. At the 21st anniversary in 1933 I remember that almost all the previous queens returned. These queens, and those crowned over the next few years, were:

1913 Kathleen Holden	1922 Hilda Halestrap	1931 Winifred Martin
1914 Winnie Cobb	1923 Betty King	1932 Vera Phythian
1915 Olive Gillings	1924 Edith Taylor	1933 Daisy Carter
1916 Ruby Roberts	1925 Betty Knight	1934 Kathleen Sorrell
1917 Phyllis Dean	1926 Betty Holden	1935 Betty Martin
1918 Marjorie Turner	1927 Doris Symes	1936 Betty ?.
1919 Phyllis Lewis	1928 Enid Berry	1937 Peggy Claydon
1920 Madge Gillings	1929 Margaret Phythian	1938 Betty Fryer
1921 Mary Mason	1930 Isabella Maclaire	1939 Marion Tipper

Two of the Rector's daughters, Kathleen (1913) and Betty (1926) were Queens, as were three pairs of sisters, Olive and Madge Gillings, Margaret and Vera Phythian, and Winifred and Betty Martin.

One of the Upminster "characters" of my younger days was Jimmy Ingleton who played an active part in the earliest May festivals dressed in a smock leading a tumbril cart pulled by Sadie, the Rectory donkey, carrying the young children dressed in their May festival finery. According to an article which I have from an old church magazine Jimmy was proud of this role and considered himself one of the features of the festival, second only to the queen herself. Born in the parish in April 1837, the year that Queen Victoria came to the throne, he was described as "simple in his ideas and tastes, very lovable and a staunch friend." Although he could neither read nor write he had a remarkable memory which was essential when he took notes round. He would place these notes in various pockets so that he delivered them at the right houses, literally carrying out his errands at a jog, wasting no time at the job in hand. Jimmy had hoped to live long enough to see the Rector return from the war but it was not to be. He died before his wish was fulfilled and was buried in the churchyard.

Jimmy Ingleton and Sadie the donkey, May Festival 1913

My grandfather George Halestrap was born at Norton Mandeville, Essex in December 1836 and came to Hornchurch around 1854 when he was seventeen years of age. When my father was born in Hornchurch in 1870, grandfather was described as a labourer in one of the village's famous iron foundries. On his death in 1929 aged 92 an obituary in the local paper described him as a "bearded but energetic figure" who was one of Hornchurch's "best known personalities", respected "as much for his natural character as his years". His main hobby was cycling and he would go for a ride every day, until he had an accident only a few years before he died. He would often travel to Romford and bring home shopping for Hornchurch residents, to save them the journey. A keen churchman, he claimed that he had attended fifty Christmas services at St Laurence Church, Upminster, although towards his latter years he was more likely to attend the closer St Andrew's, Hornchurch. He had a very good memory and was a person who rarely forgot faces or facts.

Grandfather believed that seven was his lucky number and would point out that he and his wife Flora (née Burgess), who had been born at the old Hornchurch millhouse, had had seven children – six boys and a single girl, Alice. In addition to my father Frederick and his brother Walter, with whom he worked, the other boys were Harry, who went out to Australia, Albert, who lived at Romford, Leonard, who died young, and Arthur, who was a policeman at Southampton. Not long after we came to Upminster I remember how exciting it was when our four cousins from Southampton, Uncle Arthur's children, came to spend their holidays with their Essex relations. The two girls would stay with Uncle Walter in North Street while the two boys would stay with my grandparents. I am still in touch with one of those cousins, Arthur (known as Bill), who is now over 100 years old and one

Hilda Halestrap with her grandfather George Halestrap

of the few remaining veterans of the First World War still able to make the trip back to the battlefields and war graves.

Uncle Walter was very active in local parish affairs in the early years of the 20th century and the books by Hornchurch's historian, Mr Perfect, contain many references to him. He was a member of the local Company of Rifle Volunteers, attached to the 15th Essex Rifle Volunteer Corps, which had been formed in Hornchurch in 1860. According to Mr Perfect, this Corps eventually became H Company of the 1st Volunteer Battalion Essex Regiment. Almost all the local company volunteered for active service when the Boer War in South Africa broke out but just seven were accepted in February 1900, among them my Uncle Walter, who was then a sergeant, and his brother Harry, a private. Both returned safely from their South African venture. Uncle Walter was one of the organising committee in September 1903 when the Hornchurch Company of the Church Lads' Brigade was formed, to provide a club for boys between 13 and 19. He became one of the Company's first officers, initially appointed as Staff Sergeant-Major, later becoming Lieutenant. As one of the local parish councillors for Hornchurch throughout the First War, Uncle Walter took an interest in the Allotment scheme. He was Chairman of the Committee that dealt with this scheme, acquiring suitable land locally and encouraging its cultivation. He was very active in public service during the war years and in 1919 was elected Vice Chairman of the parish council.

My grandparents Halestrap lived at Vine Cottage on Butts Green Road, Hornchurch, close to where the junction with Hillview Avenue now is. They moved there around the 1890s

Ernie, Hilda and Fred Halestrap with Rev Holden, May Festival 1936

when grandfather took early retirement from Romford Brewery on account of my grand-mother's illness (it was said in his obituary that he worked at the Brewery for 35 years). Grandmother died during the war years, after which my aunt Alice, his only daughter, looked after him. Until two weeks before he died in 1929 he had been in good health but was then confined to bed with bronchial trouble. He sensed that his end was near and got up from his bed two days before he died to sit in a favourite seat in front of the fire of the living room. After grandfather's death Aunt Alice married but she had no children.

My father was a keen gardener and a long-standing member of the Upminster Horticultural Society. He always took part in the society's shows and won many cups for his efforts. He was also a member of the Romford Horticultural Society, whose shows were held in the hall behind the Kings Head in the market place. On one occasion he decided to enter a rather large aspidistra in their show. Having no car in those days we travelled by train to Romford. My brother Ernie was put in charge of the aspidistra and in the train, with all eyes on Ernie and the aspidistra, he whispered to me "I don't know why Dad had to put this old thing in the show". Arriving at the hall we placed out entries, the aspidistra taking up more than its fair share of room in the space allocated to house plants. The next evening we returned to collect our winnings, if any, and to bring the exhibits home. To our amazement the aspidistra won not only first prize in its section but a special certificate, much to my father's delight, but Ernie and I just kept quiet. Dad picked up his winnings, had a chat with one or two friends and we left for home, Ernie and the aspidistra once more the focus of attention on the train. After we arrived home the aspidistra was returned to its usual place on a table in the front room window. But alas, in a few weeks it began to wilt and change colour and in a short while collapsed and died. The journey and publicity had been just too much for it! This incident was a family joke for many years which, after a while, even my father appreciated.

His brother Walter, whom father worked with, died in 1923 when he was still quite young, aged only around 46 or 47, and the business was sold after my father decided not to carry on with it. My cousin Barbara, Walter's daughter, continued to live at their house in North Street. She was two years younger than me and we were great pals. She was well known in local musical circles as a teacher of singing and piano, and was well loved, both for herself and her musical abilities. She died suddenly in 1979, aged 72, after which the adjacent Frosts motors bought the house in North Street.

Upminster Hockey teams, 1925

The Glebe Tennis Club was also popular, and the Rector in particular was an accomplished player. My main sport was hockey. I joined the local club in 1925, playing as centre half through until the war, and at times I was team captain. Our local rivals were Hornchurch, who we were always delighted to beat, as there was some rivalry when we played, particularly as some members of both teams had attended Romford County High School together. Our hockey fixtures took us all around the neighbouring areas, out as far as Fairlop. I remember one Saturday match there well when I got a cut above the eye. With blood pouring down my face I was taken into a tent where a doctor was in attendance. He promptly lit a cigarette, gave it to me and told me to smoke it to calm me down! I think that's what started me off on the habit! I arrived home at teatime (I remember that it was shrimps and winkles!) with my head swathed in bandages. The family took one look at me and resumed eating without saying a word, although their looks showed that they thought I had it coming for playing this sport. I sat down and cried my eyes out. On the following Monday, with the bandages removed and a plaster over my wound, I turned up for work to comments such as "And how's the other chap?"

The St Laurence Dramatic Society, which I joined in 1930, was another of my pastimes. This had been founded by a Mr R H Roberts around the first war. Not only did he paint the scenery but I think he also wrote one or two of the plays which we performed. But more usually our performances were of better-known plays, including some by Ian Hay, a popular playwright of the times. I recall playing the Admiral's wife in a naval play, "The Middle Watch" and also remember a play on an army theme, called "Orders is Orders". We performed two plays each year, with two performances of each, on Thursdays and Saturdays, at the St Laurence Church Hall. Mr Copley printed the programmes, at his printing works in the basement of his ironmonger's shop in Station Road. Performances were posh affairs, with the stewards and programme sellers attired in evening dress! I have two extracts from the programmes for the Society's productions from the early 1920s. The programme for "The Waster", which seems to date from late 1922, shows a play in three acts produced (and possibly written) by Mr R H Roberts, who himself played two parts. It is interesting to note that the three female actresses were all May Queens: Kathleen Holden (1913), Olive Gillings (1915) and Marjorie Turner (1918). For many years my brother kept a book of cuttings of the Society's activities. Where this is now, I don't know but, if it still exists, what memories must be within its pages.

My father counted Mr Copley among his many good friends. He would sometimes mind the ironmonger's shop while Mr Copley went to the bank or post office on business. The unmarried Mr Copley had a large collection of gramophone records and father would visit him in the evening sometimes to listen to some of them. Mr Copley's sister was a Mrs Moore, whose son was killed in the first war.

The Second World War brought sadness to our family as in August 1941 my younger brother Ernie was killed in action while serving with the Royal Air Force aged 26. He was a rear gunner in a Wellington bomber shot down over Holland. His grave, in a cemetery near Flushing, was adopted by a local Dutch family named Crucq and for many years we used to pay regular visits there. Although I have not made the trip to Holland for many years, I still keep in touch by telephone with their daughter, Riet, now in her eighties.

"The Waster,"

A Comedy in Three Acts.

Characters (in order of appearance) :

Clarice Aveley	Marjorie Turner
Mary Steele	Olive Gillings
Lawson (a butler)	R. H. Roberts
Henry (a page boy)	Harold Cullum
Laurence Pountney	H. Robert Roberts
Maurice Aveley	L. W. Oram
Lady Aveley	Kathleen Holden
Sir George Aveley, M.P.... ...	T. C. Mulinder
Walker (a policeman)	Harold Cullum
Harris (the Town Hall keeper) ...	W. Leslie Ivey
The Mayor of Market Bloxham ...	R. H. Roberts

Act I.—Sir George Aveley's Library.

Act II.—The same,—a year later.

Act III.—The Mayor's Parlour in the Town Hall, Market Bloxham,—eighteen months later.

The Play produced by Mr. R. H. ROBERTS.

Wigs by HUGO.   Costumes by WALLER.

Business Manager   ...   Mr. H. R. ROBERTS.

ENTR'ACTE MUSIC,
Under the direction of Mr. R. WESTON.

March	": Amazonen "	*Von Blon*
Selection	"Cabaret Girl "	*Kern*
Selection	" Mayfair and Montmartre "	
Suite	" Rebel Maid "	*Phillips*

Cast list for St Laurence Dramatic Society production "The Waster", 1922

Halestrap family in the late 1930s

In her later years mother was not very mobile as she had trouble with her legs. But although she was not able to get about much, she always did her best to keep active, knitting and mending, writing letters to friends and relations and carrying out such household chores as she could, such as cleaning the silver each week. Shortly after the war in 1947 my mother died but my father survived her by nine years, dying in June 1956, aged 85. The following year my brother Fred and I decided to move from 23 St Lawrence Road, our home for over 48 years, as we felt it was time for a change. We then moved to the house where I now live in Cranborne Gardens. After I retired from my job in 1964 I found no shortage of interests to pursue. I joined the Upminster Art Society and my cousin Barbara's afternoon ladies choir and, like my father, I entered the Horticultural Society's flower shows.

I suppose I can thank my father and grandfather, for I seem to have inherited their long lives. These days my hearing is not very good and my sight is failing but I still have my memories, and I have to be thankful for a long and happy life spent in Upminster.

Upminster February 2000

PRETTY MAY FESTIVAL

The annual May festival held in Upminster by St Laurence Church is an event which, by virtue of its gorgeousness, is calculated to leave a deep and lasting impression on the minds of the children who participate and also the crowds of the general public who witness it. That which was held on Saturday was no less effective than its nine predecessors, and the brilliant light of the summer sun emphasised the brightly-coloured silks and satins worn by the "Queens"and their attendants and courts. The setting being in an old-fashioned village where, with the exception of an occasional omnibus, the aspect in all directions is of the "truly rural" order, was entirely appropriate and suitable, and a better place than the Rectory grounds for the crowning ceremony could not have been found.

Crowning of Hilda Halestrap as May Queen, 1922

The excitement among the children and also among those interested in them had been maintained for a long period by the preparations, and on Saturday it rose to its height as, headed by the Hornchurch Cottage Homes Band, the whole of the dignified procession of ex- "Queens" made their way through the village. There were Misses Mary Mason ("Queen" in 1921), Madge Gillings (1920), Phyllis Lewis (1919), Marjorie Turner (1918), Kathleen Holden (1913), all of Upminster; and the Misses Edith Fenn, Beatrice Gardiner, Lucy Olley, Margaret Collard, of Barking, who were followed by Eric Moore, the Prime Minister, and numerous "ladies-in-waiting," who were all hardly less beautifully dressed.

"Queen" Mary, who was elected in 1921 and was due to abdicate this year in favour of Miss Hilda Halestrap, extended a hearty and suitable ceremonious welcome to "Queen"

Edith of Barking. After this she resigned her throne, and was presented with a gold brooch and crowned with a wreath of forget-me-nots, to the obvious approval of the gay cavaliers, her pages, Donald Raven and Ernest Halestrap, and her nine Old English maids-of-honour. The banner bearer throughout the ceremonies was Allan Nicholls, and the crown bearer was George Townsend.

After the proclamation had been read by the "Prime Minister," another procession of the "Queens" and attendants took place, and upon their arrival, again in the grounds the Rector of Upminster (the Rev. H.H. Holden) crowned the new "Queen".

The paying of the homage was a particularly pretty sight, and both in this and in their general behaviour ample evidence was given of the capital training given to the children by Miss Coles, of Barking, and other ladies of Upminster who supervised them.

The latter part of the afternoon was given up to May Day revels led off, as usual, by a musical selection. The infants indulged in some charming games, but the chief items perhaps were the country dances which, with the costumes worn, were most effective. Miss McFarlane gave a solo dance and the May Queens a "stately measure".

Upminster connections

Brian Moore

The Rowe family grocery business was established in about the middle of the nineteenth century at the Cosy Corner, though this name came later. This central location opposite the Bell Inn and on the main crossroads was best suited for the grocery trade but the premises proved to be inadequate and the business was moved to premises on Upminster Hill, which were converted to retail uses. The Rowe family also had a shoemaking business, which was carried on in a one-storied building on the west side (downhill) of "Ivy House", two doors past the Upminster Hill shop. Some of the staff were employed canvassing for orders - customers' feet were measured on the spot!

The shop on the hill had been added to an earlier house, part of which was converted to retail use. The upper storerooms still retained a blocked door and windows into the older house. Chapman and André's map of 1777 shows no building on that site, so it must have been built later than that date.

My mother Alice Ethel Rowe (1885-1967), who was granddaughter of the founder George Rowe, was born and lived at "Ivy House". About the time of her birth her father William Frederic Rowe (1850-1939) took over the village inn at Plaxtol in Kent. Mother always revered the name "Plaxtol", as her mother Amy Alice (née West) died there in 1887 and was buried in the churchyard. She gave this name to our house, when we moved up to 2 Stewart Avenue, Upminster in 1930. Mother had a brother, Reginald who died young and unmarried.

My mother told me that her grandfather George Rowe was responsible for the planting of the yew avenues at St Laurence church, after it was rebuilt in 1862. She said that her father, then aged 12, helped to fill in the holes when the trees were planted. This yew avenue replaced an earlier avenue of chestnut trees, one of which, I recall, was still there in the 1930s. Her grandfather Rowe found he had three trees left over, and planted them in the garden of the shop, where they were used to screen the outdoor lavatory! When I was a child I found the branches very useful for making bows! The trees survived until the whole area was demolished, about 1957.

The same George Rowe, who died in 1901, and his wife Betsey Jessie, who died in 1915, both at the advanced age of 91 according to their tombstone in Upminster churchyard, lie under a tall Saxon cross near the wall before you come to the war memorial. When last seen by me it was near to toppling, owing to the roots of the nearby flowering cherry tree which, I understand, has since been felled leaving only the stump.

Yew Avenue, leading to Upminster Church, c.1917

Below: *Wedding party of Harold Moore and Alice Rowe, 1 July 1907. Standing: ?,?, Reg Rowe, Harold Moore, Alice Rowe, Maud and Ada Rowe, William F Rowe. Seated: George West and wife, Mrs Betsey Rowe and Mrs Jessie Baker. On floor: ?,?, Katharine & Edith Baker. The photograph was taken at "Ivy House", Upminster and the background shows the shop garden, with greenhouses containing vines of Black Hamburgh grapes.*

According to family tradition the Rowes came to Upminster late in the seventeenth century. They originated from John, the younger son of John Rowe, lord of the manor of Staverton, near Totnes, Devon. He was apprenticed to a London goldsmith named Backwell and later went into business on his own account. He was one of the victims of Charles II's closure of the Exchange in 1672, when all his cash, about £7,000, was confiscated. He was bankrupted, and like others, imprisoned. He appears to have died there, hence the ambiguous reference on the tomb in Upminster churchyard which refers only to his memory, with no details of his birth or death. His wife Mary is recorded on the tomb as having been buried in the vault beneath in 1732, in her eighty-second year. This tomb also records that they had some 16 children, 11 sons and 5 daughters.

Their son Samuel was also a goldsmith by patrimony, the progenitor of a family who still are (or were until the 1950s) active members of the society. A member of the family migrated to Newcastle in the early 1900s and became a member of the Northern Goldsmiths Company. I have a knife, given to my mother, inscribed "N. Goldsmith's Silver Jubilee, 1935". Samuel established the family's country home at Upminster, with a house now called Tadlows and small park where the entrance of Cranston Park Avenue now is. The goldsmith Rowes did not live permanently at Upminster but, like many merchants of the time, they lived mainly "over the shop".

Despite their limited residence the family used the vault in the churchyard, no doubt after burial rites in town, the last burial there being Nicholas Rowe in 1816. A massive iron railing surrounded the tomb, which bears the arms of the Thomas Rowe family impaling those of his wife. This was quite intact until World War Two when, without so much as a "by your leave", the authorities removed the rails, apparently to throw at Hitler, damaging the roll-moulding. Mother was furious, but to no avail (I was in the desert at the time).

At Upminster Hall, during the days when the Branfill family still lived there, there was a portrait of Thomas Rowe and son, acquired by the family at some time. My mother saw it during visits and was able to recall it in detail. There was a strong belief in our family that the portrait was by Gainsborough. I know for sure that the work was executed at Bath where the family had gone to "take the waters". Until recently I had doubted the Gainsborough connection but I now understand that Thomas Gainsborough lived and worked in Bath from 1759 to 1774 - which may well add credence to the family belief. It is strange that the picture was not included in the sale of the Hall, as an uncle who obtained a copy of the sale catalogue ascertained, but appears to have been disposed of privately. If there be any truth in the belief in its origin, the picture has probably disappeared long since into an American collection.

How the portrait came to be hanging in the Branfill's home I'm not aware. As far as I know the Rowes had no link to the Branfills, although there is a connection in so far as both families have Devon origins. I have been told that the Branfills were descended from a very ancient Devon family by the name of Bampfylde. During the reign of Charles II a son (Andrew) obtained a license, called "letters of marque", from the king to arm a private ship of war, with which he was based at Plymouth. Captain Branfill preyed successfully on the merchant ships of the countries with whom we were at war - Holland, France

Upminster Hall, home of the Branfill Family

and Spain - making so much from the sale of the spoils that he soon retired. Realising that the source of his wealth was known locally in Devon, he came to Upminster and established a family at the hall, which they held for over 200 years. It became the family tradition to name their eldest son "Champion", which I found was the name of his private ship.

My father Harold Alfred Moore (1878-1975) originated from Gravesend, where he was born. He was apprenticed to Mr William H. Rowe, my great-uncle, at the Upminster shop in February 1893. It is a curious fact that Dad's father carried out a substantial shoe factory at Gravesend and it may well be that Dad came to Upminster to learn that trade in the Rowe's shoemaking business, converting to the Rowe's other trade - the grocers' business - when the sudden death of his father compelled the sale of the business. This is only speculation but I feel it may be right.

My father would gleefully tell an anecdote relating to the Branfill family. Mrs Branfill would drive down each week to the grocers' shop on Upminster Hill but would never go in. It was Dad's job to attend to the side of the carriage and take down her order. On one occasion, while Dad was taking down Mrs Branfill's order, one of the horses suddenly sneezed, and then back-fired! Mrs Branfill did not turn a hair. "Poor dear", she said, "he must have got a cold, both ends"- and continued reading out the order, as usual. Mrs Branfill was the last of the family at the Hall and was something of a character. She kept a clothes-basket full of skulls and other human bones in the hall to horrify or amuse visitors. These bones had been dug up over the years on the site and area of the former chapel. This had dated to the time when the monks of Waltham Abbey used to be retired to the Hall, when they were no longer able to stand the rigorous monastic life.

During World War One my father served with the Royal Garrison Artillery, being invalided out in early 1918 and spending the rest of the year in a wheelchair at a large country house in Suffolk. Working the guns in a sea of mud in France was the cause of his leg trouble. The shop was taken over on the death of Mr W H Rowe by my great-uncle Charles H. Baker, who was a grocer in Hornchurch and prominent there in local civic affairs. Mr Baker, who was married to my great aunt, Jessie Rowe, had bought the business for his son but the latter was killed at Gallipoli in 1915. As a result of the loss of his son Mr Baker sold the business to the brewers Whitbread at the end of the war, as they were no doubt adding the off licence trade which formed part of the shop into their holdings. In the early 1930s the shop was sold by Whitbreads to my father, who from 'prentice had become manager and finally owner. The business also offered hardware items such as quart sized tin kettles, priced 6d. each and there was also a millinery department, discontinued when my father took over. Dad used to issue a price-list showing the range of goods sold in his shop. Despite the fact that this was the time when the pound had the world's best purchasing value, the customers still moaned, as they always do. Australian butter, for instance, was a shilling a pound (goodness knows what the farmer got for his milk!). Apart from his service in the First World War my father continued at the shop until he retired in 1957 after 65 years in the business and aged 79. He then only retired when I decided that suburban life was not for me, and took a business at Earls Colne, north Essex.

Charlie Baker's shop on Upminster Hill, c.1912

I was born on 16 September 1914, at the house next to the shop, where we lived when father was manager. When he went into the army we had to make room for the new manager, and we moved into a house in St Lawrence Road, of which I have only a few

Brian Moore as a young child c.1917 .

scrappy memories, such as the anti-aircraft gun which was erected on a great base of railway sleepers at the junction with Garbutt Road. This fired ineffectually at the German aircraft raiders which in 1918 succeeded the Zeppelins. Its only achievement was to drop several unexploded shells near Rainham, which caused some damage. Mother spoke afterwards of the night all were brought to their doors by the sounds of jubilation coming across the fields from Hornchurch airfield, where a young pilot was being fêted after shooting down in flames an airship which had attacked London. He earned a V.C. for his feat, which had involved taking off and finding his way back to an unlit airfield.

In the top end of the cart-shed by the shop was kept a large barrel of black treacle. This was a popular item then and I loved it, spread thickly on bread'n'butter. The treacle was sold for 4*d* in jam-jars, covered with greaseproof paper and string. One Saturday, by accident or design, the slide-tap on the barrel was left partly open. On Monday, when the vanmen went to fetch the carts they were found to be standing in a shallow lake of treacle. It took several loads of gravel to absorb the glutinous mess, which consolidated as if it were tarmac! I was severely questioned over the treacle affair, but could honestly say "I didn't do it!" One of the vanmen, who lived in the Post Office Cottages on Corbets Tey Road near where Swan Libraries now is, was known to all as "Bubbo", because he whistled and hummed, *ad nauseam*, a hit of the day called *I'm forever blowing bubbles* (now the theme tune of West Ham Football Club). He was a melancholy type, like the song, which I can still recall, both words and music.

Mr Ernest "Tiny" Gates, the estate agent, was related in some way or other to us, maybe through the Bakers where he was often to be found. At one time he was believed to have a crush on one of the Baker daughters, Kathy or her sister (both of whom however later died unmarried). He was a frequent visitor at the hill and I recall him so clearly: very tall, with very thin legs, accentuated by the fact that he habitually wore plus-fours. In the distance his extremities were invisible and he seemed, therefore, to be hanging from a sky-hook!

One day, passing through the kitchen on my way down to my friend Lenny's, I saw Mr Gates' trilby hat on the kitchen table. Thinking to have fun I took it and put it in the oven of the kitchen range, oblivious to the fact that the stove was alight. Some time later my mother, trying to trace a curious smell, observed a trickle of smoke coming out of the oven top. Opening the door, she saw the trilby enveloped in a cloud of smoke. It seemed intact but when she removed it the brim fell off! I received a good beating when I came home and was docked of my pocket-money to pay for a new one. Uncle Ernie, as we called him, took it surprisingly well and, hearing later of my financial stress, slipped me half-a-crown, unobserved. He was very popular in the village and, being a bachelor, was given the glad eye by many of the village spinsters. The lady who ran the sweet shop next to his office in Station Road eventually captured him. It was a standing joke at the time when a Gates' customer wished to see him it was necessary for one of the staff to go next door and fetch him out. When he retired they went to live in Kent, and we lost touch with them. Some years later in 1969 when I sold my bungalow in Bridge Avenue Mr Parish told me that Mr Gates was still alive, although over 80.

Our shop cat "Weeny" used to sit on the ridge of the shop roof, to bask in the morning sun. Once she slipped off of a frosty roof and fell into the yard, breaking a forefoot. At the vet's surgery she lay perfectly still, purring loudly, while the vet shaved her leg, and applied bandage and plaster. She survived many years after, but never again went on that roof. Dad entered the charge "Repairs to cat, 10/-". Queried by the accountant, this was allowed on being assured that Weeny was an accredited member of the staff!

Harold Moore's grocers, Upminster Hill c1933, a few years after the shop was extended

I used to hate Sundays. I was inserted into best shorts and jacket and had fastened round my neck a deep starched white collar, which threatened to cut my throat. Enduring the jeers of friends on the way to the "Ingy" (the Ingrebourne) I proceeded to Mr Taylor's Bible class at 11 a.m., where peashooters were confiscated at sight. This took place in the "Old British School" near the bakery. After an hour of this, home to dinner, after which I was closely inspected, dirty finger-marks removed from the collar, and sent to the Rector's Sunday School, in the church. After tea I was supposed to go with my parents to the Evensong service, but usually managed, sometimes with Dad's connivance, to slip over the back wall, down the field to my friend Lenny Nice (see below), and so away into the woods.

I was sent to a private school in Emerson Park, run by an ex-Cambridge Don, Mr Woode, who after supervising morning prayers attired in black gown and mortar-board hat, retired to continue long-term experiments on the effects on his constitution of Whitbread's Pale Ale, four quarts of which were delivered weekly by dad's shop with his groceries. We pupils had lots of fun there, but all I acquired was a lasting interest in history, and the ability to discharge ink-stained darts with considerable accuracy. We travelled on the branch line (fare 3*d* return) which still runs from Upminster to Romford; it was in those times a steam locomotive, a gallant 4-4-2.

My grandfather W.F. Rowe told me that when he was a young man he used to, at a certain season of the year, set "night-lines", as he called them, to hang from the bridge into the brook. At that time migrating eels came up the Ingrebourne and for two or three days he caught several. On one occasion, he found a dab hooked, which must have come all the way up from the Thames. A hundred yards below the bridge was the remains of a gravelled ford, from which the track still remained which led to the site of Bridge Farm. In my time this was a set of crumbling walls, within the L-shaped remains of a moat. All this now probably lies beneath the gardens of Bridge Avenue.

I was much interested in the occasional visit of a Foden steam-wagon, which would stop on the bridge over the brook, the driver then lowering a pipe into the water in order to replenish his supply. We were sometimes allowed to shovel coals into the fire-box, to be rewarded by a toot on the whistle as he went.

Rummaging one day in a cupboard at home I found a package which contained a Webley revolver, which Dad had somehow kept from his war service. Caught in the act, my ears were well boxed. Dad later took it down to the brook and threw it as far as he could upstream where, no doubt, it still lies, deep in the mud.

At the top of the hill, recessed from the road by a small field stood (and I'm told still stands) Upminster windmill, in the occupation of Mr Alfred Abraham, the miller. My elder brother Eric (1908-1990) and I had never seen it working, and were very excited one day in the early 1920s to be invited to witness it in operation. We were taken to an upper floor and saw the great shaft revolving, and gazed, spellbound, at the great cogs, some of which were of wood. The rumble of the whole machinery caused the mill to wobble like a jelly. We were shown the millstones working, and were told that they came from France, which was apparently the source of the best stones to be had. We went home thrilled, and covered in a white dust. We never saw it working again.

The miller had a horse, kept in the adjoining field, that he used to pull a trap, in which he sallied forth occasionally on business. All the villagers knew this horse as the "Plate-Rack", on account of his protruding ribs. Poor thing, it could have done with some good feeds of oats, but seemed to subsist only on the tough couch-grass which infested the field. Another Mr Abraham, "Sid" (Sidney), brother of the above, was the village baker on the

Upminster Windmill in the 1930s

left in Station Road just past Aggiss' garage. An entry between led to some cottages which stood by the edge of what once had been the village green. The bakery oven, which was an old brick affair, closed by a wooden shutter, produced bread, the like of which I have never encountered since. I was often sent out for a loaf, which consisted of a large round base, plus a smaller one baked on the top: we called it a cottage loaf, a type which I believe has long since vanished in the area. It had a delicious, crisp crust, much of which I fear I consumed on the way home. Mr Abraham hardly made a living, and had no capital to have a modern oven built. Unfortunately Hornchurch Council officials harassed the poor man so much that he took his own life in the early 1950s.

Below where our shop was located, at the bottom of the hill, was a row of cottages, formerly the almshouses of the village (nowadays these still survive known as Ingrebourne Cottages). They had became derelict and were bought in the 1830s by one of my family, George Rowe, and converted to six separate cottages. The cottage at the bottom end of the row formerly had an eighteenth century fire mark in the wall. A thirties collector bought and removed this.

Sidney Abraham, outside his bakers shop

Looking east down Upminster Hill, with the chapel on the left

In the cottage at the upper end lived Mr and Mrs Nice who had two sons, the younger of whom, "Lenny", was my boon companion. Mr Nice was a labourer who died when I was quite small. In spite of her poverty Mrs Nice was a jolly person, always laughing and joking. She used to come to the shop to spend the few pennies that she had on odd pieces of bacon. Dad used to keep the bacon bones for her, with which she made stews and soups for the family. At the end of June each year she was to be observed, dressed in her best, making her way up to the "Old Chapel", which stands near the top of the hill, and attending the Sunday service therein. The congregation, a rather austere sect, hired a *char-a-banc* each August for an annual outing, usually to Southend or Clacton. Mrs Nice, by virtue of her attendance, always claimed a seat, arriving early to make sure. After the event her attendances at the Sunday services became noticeably fewer, soon fading away altogether, until next June! We used to laugh at her antics, but understood it was the only holiday she ever had.

A regular passer-by of the shop in the weekdays for several years in the 1920s was "Tiny" Thompson. He was short, elderly and brisk in manner. He was always attended by two small white "Scotties", firmly held in a double leash. He invariably passed our house at 10.05 a.m. - you could have set the clock by him. Destination? The *Bridge House* Inn. On arrival he would secure the dogs outside, where they would resignedly settle down for a long wait. Upon the midday closure he would emerge, rather unsteady, uncouple the dogs, who evidently knew what they were brought for, and they would set off for home at a brisk pace, dragging Mr Thompson behind. We used to watch for him to appear, very often staggering sideways at the end of the leash. He was supposed to come from the part of Upminster known to us always as "over the bridge" (the area to the north of the station). We assumed that he came so far in order that his familiars should not observe his lubrications!

I well remember the muffin man patrolling the streets of Upminster in the early 1920s. Tall, of a military bearing, he arrived at the station from town, travelling in the guard's van with a long tray, balanced on a small round cushion on his head. This, covered with a white cloth, was filled with muffins, round, white and about an inch or so deep. After walking slowly round, occasionally ringing a brass handbell, and selling of his stock as much as he could, he would come down the hill. We used to look out for him, and persuade mother to buy. He passed on up the hill to Hornchurch and the cook at the house called Dury Falls at the corner of Wingletye Lane often bought the rest of his stock, whereupon he walked down to Hornchurch station, and so away. He was certainly a gentleman, in speech and manners. It's three-quarters of a century since he passed from my ken, but I can still recall the delicious flavour and texture of the muffins. We used to impale them on toasting-forks, hold them close to the glowing coals of the fire until browned and piping hot, and cover them with butter.

Opposite the shop was a large house, later a Royal Engineers, Territorial Army Drill Hall (the local corps was mobilised as a searchlight unit at the outbreak of war in 1939 and stationed for much of it in the Essex coastal marshes). The gardens of this house (which was occupied by a family named Preston-Hillary) stretched down as far as what is now Bridge Avenue and were bounded by a high brick wall, on the road side of which were a row of

Looking down Upminster Hill towards Hornchurch, with the Drill Hall on the left

pollarded trees. Within the wall, about six feet from it, was a pronounced grassy bank, probably the original boundary of the road. Digging a path across this, the gardener found a coin, which he took across to my father, who gave him half-a-crown for it. Years later, a customer's husband identified it as a Roman "sestertius", which being in quite good condition, he gave Dad something for it. Proof, perhaps, of the antiquity of the road, which some believe to have been a late Roman road to the eroded site of the Saxon Shore fort of Shoeburyness. When the brick wall was taken down the cap-stones on the many pillars were found to have been cut from gravestones, circa 1800, the inscriptions, face down, quite clear. When "Hill House" was renovated, preparatory to it becoming a school, a workman found in the eaves a rolled up, yellow eighteenth century news-sheet, called, I think, *The Post Boy*. The finder claimed it, so I don't know what became of it.

I can clearly recollect the May Queen Festival of '22 when Hilda Halestrap was crowned queen. My elder brother Eric was Hilda's Prime Minister (aged 14½)! I was just a looker-on! Uncle ("Daddy") West used to come and lecture we boys, standing in front of the fire and, on one occasion, on the cat's tail too! My grandmother was a West, who died young, and so my mother was brought up by her gran'ma, who lived to a great age, dying 1916. I remember the Eldred's smithy, although it was closed by my time. I bought my sweets at the Cosy Corner - liquorice boot-laces, a half-penny each! I remember how they used to close the path in front of the Cosy Corner once a year, in order to prevent it becoming a right-of-way. Playing by the Ingrebourne, and picking armfuls of bluebells in the woods where Aldboro' Road now is! My mother could remember when she used to pick violets and primroses up Hall Lane!

On the way to the Common, where the arterial road to Southend now runs, was formerly a spring beside the road, with delicious ever-flowing cold water, which we drank from

48

cupped hands, and splashed over our heads and faces. Dr Derham, a former rector in the late seventeenth century, mentioned that it was in being in his day, although he was of the impression that springs derived from the sea! When later the Arterial was double-tracked, this was cut back into the bank. The latter was of stiff yellow clay which, by some geological freak, enclosed a "pipe" of sand, down which the water continued to flow. It was finally destroyed, I think, when the later fly-over was built.

Hall Lane, close to junction with Ashburnham Gardens c.1917

Just a little way off Bird Lane there was formerly a brick-works, long abandoned. We heard one day that the great kiln was to be demolished, so eagerly went to see. The workmen knocked holes at intervals round it, and put charges behind the surviving parts. Having shooed us to a safe distance, the kiln was brought down with a most satisfactory crash, covering everybody with brick-dust. Many came down to salvage whole bricks, which were dark red, and of a quality and character contrasting greatly with the lifeless "Phorpres" bricks of today.

Our pleasures were simple, and home made. Besides bows and arrows, we fixed butter-boxes on old pram wheels and raced each other down the hill. I fear my greatest pleasure was to explode key-bombs behind the elderly, making them jump through their hats, and being pursued with shouts of "You little devil, I'll tell your father". Our (unpatented) recipe for key bombs was as follows.

1. Take an old-fashioned key of good length, with a long hollow shank.
2. Loosely fit a nail (6" ideal), first filing down the point to a smooth flat end.
3. Tie a loop of string from the nail-head to the key handle.
4. Scrape the heads of three or four matches into the shank.
5. Tamp the same into the key.
6. Swing the assembly - nail-head first - against a wall or pavement
7. Explosion!

I remember Upminster when it was a pleasant country village. When it became a town I wanted to get away, and was lucky to manage it. Looking back in age, down the vista of the years - and possibly through the wrong end of a telescope - they seem to have been golden times when my friend Lenny and I adventured into a still unspoilt countryside, armed with packets of bread-butter-jam sandwiches and stone bottles of Macarthy's ginger beer (real stuff in those days, it scoured the throat). We fished and splashed in a bright, unpolluted Ingrebourne, our beloved "Ingy", we challenged each other to climb the tall elms, we searched the tall hedges for rare birds' nests, we blackberried, I plunged into prickly bushes to get the fruit for Dad's sloe gin. When we got cycles we travelled far afield to Belhus Park in the south, and in the north to the splendid site of Thorndon Old Hall, where we sat on the grassy mound which once held the summer-house, and looked out over the Essex flats to the Thames and the hills of Kent, beyond.

Such were our days, in a countryside of peace and quiet, now vanished for ever.

Oslo, Norway. May 2000

Hacton in the 1920s

Peter Hills

I was born on 3 March 1917 at Park Corner Farm, Hacton the home of my grandfather Knight, and I lived there until we moved to 14 Garbutt Road in about 1920. My mother died in April 1922 and from then on my older brother John and I spent a considerable time — particularly at holidays — at Park Corner Farm.

My earliest memories include having a boiled egg for breakfast and smashing the inverted empty shell in my egg cup. I also remember being sat on the copper next to the large stone sink to be washed. At that time people came down from the east end of London to work at the farm for pea and bean picking. They were put up in the large barn, sleeping on beds made with hurdles. One day, while I was sat on the copper being washed, I came out with some language not fit for a child which I had picked up from our temporary visitors: needless to say I was banned from the pea-pickers' company from that point on.

Painting of Park Corner Farm by S Richardson, May 1926

51

My favourite occupation at the farm was to accompany one of the farm hands, Sam Peters, when he fed the chickens and collected eggs. As the hens were truly free range and roamed over a wide area, hunting for eggs was like a treasure hunt. There were two dogs that I can recall well: Jock the Retriever was the "yard dog" and Spider the whippet, the only dog allowed indoors. Another vivid memory was a nighttime visit to the W.C. — an old-fashioned cesspit located half-way up the back garden. My Aunt May (mother's sister) couldn't have been exactly pleased to stand outside in the pitch dark holding a candle, waiting for my brother John and I to complete our visit!

When we stayed on the farm we slept in what was known as "Mr Millington's Room". We never found out who George Millington was, perhaps a friend of Aunt May killed in the First World War. The other small bedroom had a small ante-room filled with copies of *Great War Illustrated* - very interesting to small boys!

As already mentioned we spent a considerable amount of time at the farm, a marvellous place for hide and seek in the numerous outhouses, sheds etc. Games of cricket were improvised in the farm yard playing with an empty petrol tin for a wicket and a sawn-off bat — this was an old cricket bat which at some time had become damaged at the bottom, which was sawn off to make a size suitable for a boy. Proper sized boys' cricket bats were an unheard of luxury but we were fortunate: close at hand across the bottom meadow were the osier beds. These willows were usually a source of wood used to fashion bows and arrows but when I was about 10 years old my Grandfather Knight had four full-size cricket bats made by Wisdens from the willow grown there. One each went to my brother John and I, while our cousins Jack and Eric Knight received the other two. I had mine for many years, even using it when I was an adult.

Of course, rides out on the farm carts were popular with us, as also was paddling and — when our female cousins weren't there — nude bathing in the Ingrebourne which we damned up with mud to provide a deep enough pool. Those taking part included cousins staying at the farm and Alf, George and Stan, sons of Joe Morant, the farm foreman.

When we were staying at the farm the visits we made to Romford on market days on Wednesdays were a popular outing as the cattle market there was fascinating to small boys. The drill was that the farmers went to market and wives went on shopping expeditions, to meet later before going home. I believe that while we were there we had a meal in Stones (Debenhams is now on this spot). From the farm when I was about seven or eight I went to the cinema for the first time, walking to the Queen's Cinema in Station Lane, Hornchurch on a Saturday morning where I saw an episode in the *Dr Fu Manchu* series, from the book written by Sax Rohmer. On walks to Hornchurch from the farm we would always stop for a drink at the spring which was located on the left just over the Ingrebourne Bridge at Hacton near to two white wooden cottages.

A few other childhood memories of days spent at Park Corner Farm come to mind. In the barn was a knife grinder – a complicated machine set on a stand, comprising a set of cogwheels activated by a handle which turned the actual grinder. One day I somehow managed to get my finger caught in these cogs and Dr Lambe was urgently summoned from

Hornchurch to tend to my wound. To this day a large scar is still visible on my finger. Another occasion which led to more disgrace was when our cousin Peggy lost her shoe in the mud at the River Ingrebourne. We gave her a piggy-back all the way home — shoe in hand — but nevertheless on arrival it was us boys who of course got the blame for her plight!

To the farming community the shooting season was the occasion for large shooting parties. Our family was no exception and all our farming relatives gathered at Park Corner Farm to take part in the grand shoot, held over grandfather's land. Grandfather's share of the birds bagged during the shoot was in due course cooked by Aunt May and served in the large dining room. I remember that roast pheasant and partridge were very tasty.

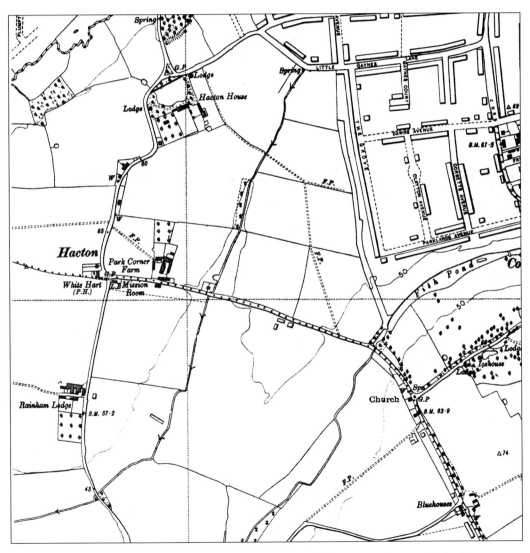

Hacton in the 1930s. The development of the Gaynes Park Estate is underway on the former manor of Gaynes, but Hacton hamlet remains unchanged from the previous decade, described in this chapter.

Hacton in the 1920s was quite a large community, remote from Upminster village. Approaching Hacton from Hacton Lane, across Hacton Bridge over the River Ingrebourne the first homes to be reached were after the junction with Little Gaynes Lane. In a house on the corner there lived Mr Irlam and just beyond this was a lodge, occupied by Mr Hayman. Past here the road bore right and then left after which a row of thatched cottages, in one of which lived Mrs Lazell, who did the Park Corner laundry.

Just beyond, on the other side of the road, were two cottages, one of which was occupied by Mr Feltham, who was the driver of the Foden Steam Wagon kept at Park Corner Farm. This grand vehicle had taken over from the large farm cart used to transport grandfather Knight's farm goods to market. This daily trip would start off from Upminster at 4 a.m. in the morning destined for the Borough Market in Southwark where grandfather had a stall bearing his name and that of his farm. All the pubs surrounding the market were open this early, serving a good breakfast as well as drinks. A selection of grandfather's best produce — peas, beans, cabbages, cauliflowers and potatoes — would be put on display for the wholesale buyers to inspect and place bulk orders. I recall that there were three kinds of potatoes: small potatoes were called "chats", medium ones "middlings", and large ones "wares". Wheat was never sold in bulk, only for horse feed. When uncle Jack Knight took over grandfather's farming business after he died, there was some dismay in the family as he gave up the outlet stall at the Borough Market.

After the cottages where Mr Feltham lived came the path which ran from Top Meadow at Park Corner Farm, across the lane and on to the River Ingrebourne. I was told that before I was born the men of Hacton had a cricket team which played at Top Meadow, and I recall that there was a building on stilts in the field there which had served as a pavilion for the cricket team. The bottom field near Gaynes lake was known appropriately as the Bottom Meadow, and the farm's horses were let out to graze here at weekends, when not being worked. Other fields at the farm were known as Frogley or Frogmore Field, and the Backlands.

Further on from the path to Top Meadow was the cottage occupied by Will Hammond, horseman at the farm, and his wife Lucy. Next was the White Hart Inn, licensee Mr Brazier, from where a penny bar of Sharp's toffee or a bar of Cadbury's chocolate could be bought at the side door. From this point the road ran on towards Rainham, first reaching Rainham Lodge, which was still within Upminster parish and was the home of William Strang, later Lord Strang. At the White Hart the road swung left past St Chad's Mission Church and on towards Park Corner Farm. Across the road from the farm entrance there was another row of cottages (in one of which I think lived a member of the Morant family, possibly 'Tommy') while just beyond the farm entrance lived Joe Morant, who was foreman there. Further down on the same side in a pair of cottages or houses by the Bottom Meadow lived Sam Peters. Sam had originally been a cowman but when we knew him he was general handyman at the farm, carrying out a range of jobs such as mending the farm boxes used to carry produce, looking after the chickens, and maintaining the items of machinery. I remember that one piece of machinery kept in the big barn on the right-hand side of the farmyard was a threshing machine (although to us it was known as a thrashing machine, no doubt reflecting the Essex accent.) The purpose of the machine was to separate the husks — the outer covering of the cereal grain — from the seeds. These husks were known as "chaff", a term, which also included chopped hay or straw, used for animal feed or bedding. After we moved away from Upminster my brother and I would visit Sam Peters on Christmas morning, taking him as a present two great big red and white spotted handkerchiefs. In the cottage beyond Sam Peters lived Mrs Letch, while the house called Chapmans (which still survives) was on the other side, further down. Other Hacton residents' names that I recall were Mrs Edmunds, who worked at Park Corner, Bateman and Cant.

Aunt May Knight at Park Corner Farm, 1920s.

As I grew older, on Sundays after the 9.30 a.m. service frequently I used to walk over after church to see Grandfather Knight at Park Corner Farm. It was a great shock to me when he died in 1928 and that era came to an end. When Aunt May left Hacton in October that year the congregation at St Chad's Mission signed a testimonial to her, commemorating "the many happy associations with the work of S.Chad's in which you and members of your family took a willing part." The names listed seem to be a roll-call of the families inhabiting the hamlet at that time:

Mrs Barnard	Mrs F Edmunds	Mr and Mrs Mays
Mrs J Bell	Mrs Gridley	Mr and Mrs Peters
Mrs Boreham	Mrs Hazelwood	Mrs Sheppard
Mrs Brown	Mrs Hardy	Mr Thedel
Mrs Brazier	Mr and Mrs Hammond	Mr H G Walker
		Hon. Organist
Mrs Bateman	Mrs Hammond Senr.	The Priest in Charge and
		Mrs Lewis
Mrs Crisp	Mr Hale	The Rector of Upminster and
		Mrs Holden
Mrs Cant	Mr and Mrs Irlam	
Mrs Crowe	Mrs Lazell	October 8 1928.
Miss K Cudby	Mrs E Lazell	
Mrs H Cudby	Mrs Letch	
Mrs A Cudby	Mr and Mrs J Morant	
Mrs Carter	Miss R Morant	
Mr and Mrs Edmunds Senr.	Miss A Morant	
Mr and Mrs G Edmunds	Mrs Morant Senr.	

Grandfather Knight had owned the house we lived in, 14 Garbutt Road (I used to walk over regularly to pay him the rent). On his death his executors sold the house, which my father bought for £420. A few years ago I saw this house for sale (asking price £120,000) — a place duly "tarted up" as per estate agent's blurb but lacking space for a garage.

I started my school career at the Infants' held in the Old British School buildings in Station Road, Upminster. Miss Fitzgerald was our headmistress, assisted by Miss Caldecourt whose family lived opposite the school, next to Talbot's garage. My memories are few and the only things I can call to mind are making baskets from raffia, learning the alphabet and how to read and print. From there with the other boys I "graduated" to the Boys' School (former National School) on the opposite side of the road. Our headmaster was F J Cox, assisted by Mrs Cullum, who lived near us at 5 Garbutt Road, and Mrs Humphries, whose speciality was music. F J had a short stick which he wielded with great effect on the palms of offenders. To teach us mental arithmetic he would haphazardly point out figures on the blackboard. Our playground games included sliding on iced puddles in wintertime and leapfrog.

Empire Day, 24 May, was a big celebration. Anyone who had a uniform, such as the cubs or scouts, wore it in the morning when we gathered for the singing of patriotic songs, such as *Three cheers for the Red, White and Blue* and *Loud round old England's rocks.* As I remember them the full words of the latter were:

Loud round old England's rocks the azure main
Uplifts her voice and sings her old refrain
The towering crags repeat in solemn tone
Britannia, rise and proudly claim thine own.

Gaynes Manor, with Jonathan Hills, gardener to Henry Joslin, in front

Upminster Court, home of Mrs A E Williams

Our Board of Governors, who included Mrs Williams of Upminster Court and Henry Joslin Esq. of Gaynes, attended the ceremony. Every year in his address Mr Joslin would refer to the people of the British Empire and in particular to "the millions and millions of people in (H)Australasia". In the afternoon we did not have to attend classes and instead we had a Punch and Judy show in the Congregational Church Hall and, on leaving, we received a bun and an orange.

Mr Abraham's shop close to the school was a favourite stopping-off place because, in addition to being a baker's, they also sold sweets. Amongst those sweets that I recall were aniseed balls at 20 for 1*d*, gob-stoppers four-a-penny and Tiger-nuts, which were a kind of ground-nut. Rosie Abraham, who I recall was a cripple and possibly a mental deficient, used to sit by the counter. We boys would kick the shop front, accompanied by our loud shouts of "Shop!", until her sister Florrie Abraham appeared from the back of the shop to serve us. Meanwhile we would watch the baker Sid Abraham baking loaves in the adjoining ovens. The Cosy Corner was also popular with us for sweets.

When funds permitted we bought comics, usually from Dales shop in Station Road. The cheapest were *Comic Cuts* and *Chick's Own* while up the range was *Tiger Tim's Weekly*, then the *Champion* and *Triumph* and a comic (probably the *Magnet*) detailing the adventures of Harry Wharton and his gang at Greyfriars School, plus the "fat owl of the Remove", Billy Bunter. We then progressed on to a magazine called *The Scout* and then *Children's Newspaper*, edited by Arthur Mee.

Upminster Broadway, outside the former Boys' School, late 1920s

Our Boys' School had a good football team and I can remember the following players from the team in around 1925 to 1927: Goalkeeper - Dick German (later wicketkeeper for Upminster Cricket Club), "Tinny" Vinton, Walter Blake, Arty (or Hearty) White, who was son of the licensee of the Mason's Arms, Jim Whiting, "Stitcher" Taylor, Ernie Carter (brother of Daisy Carter, one of the May Queens, and he was killed in World War Two) and "Licky" Pink, whose father was chauffeur to Henry Aggiss.

My main school friends were: Cyril Pratt, who was the son of Joe Pratt, the Upminster Cricket Club scorer who lived at 1 Garbutt Road; Bert Lee from Howard Road; Bob Whitby, from St Lawrence Road who was a fellow choir boy, as was Johnnie Jupp, the butcher's son.

From the Boys' School in 1927 I won a scholarship and went to Royal Liberty School in Romford; my grandfather bought my first uniform. As a scholarship boy I was entitled to free rail travel from Upminster to Romford and then from Romford to Gidea Park, but I preferred to go to school with my friends Kirkwood and C Hall, who both lived in Hall Lane. We took the train to Emerson Park Halt (12*d* return) and then walked via The Drill to Balgores Lane and then to Royal Liberty School at Hare Hall. After two years we moved to Grays and I transferred to Palmer's School, Grays (incidentally Charlie Kydd who had been a fellow choir boy at Upminster went to school here; he was later a Squadron Leader and bomber pilot who was killed in action in World War Two).

In our spare time there were many pastimes to keep us occupied, each of which had its season. Those I can recall are: hopscotch and skipping for girls; hoops; conkers; five stones; marbles; spinning tops of which there were three kinds — Carrots, Mushrooms and peg tops — each with a distinctive shape which their name described; and blackberrying, in the autumn. In about March each year in the run up to the Oxford and Cambridge boat race there was growing excitement and we would all sport boat race favours to show our allegiance, my support being with Cambridge. Girls would wear a small celluloid doll on their lapels, dressed in either light or dark blue while we boys would wear favours, brooches or badges often in the shape of a boat which we bought from Dales or the Bonanza for a penny or half-penny. We would take our rods and fish for sticklebacks and other small fish found in the Clockhouse Lake. We would play football and cricket and climb trees in the Rectory Fields (which later became the Recreation Ground), and walk as far as Upminster Common, sometimes stopping off just over the Arterial Road (now the A127) to drink from the spring there — clear water surrounded by a wooden case. We would also walk from St Mary's Lane under the arch of the main line railway and follow the disused rail track leading to the old closed brickfields at Bird Lane. My Great Aunt Amelia Sparrow lived in one room in a house on the corner of Bird Lane and we were expected to pay her a duty visit taking groundsel for her canary. Our reward was a slice of caraway seed cake and a cup of homemade lemonade. Another duty visit was to go to Sunday tea to my Hills grandparents at Tadlows, which included hymn singing, accompanied by Auntie Helen (Dad's sister) on the piano.

Grandfather Hills (Jonathan) was gardener to Mr Joslin at Gaynes, until the latter's death.

After his retirement he was asked by his brother-in-law Jack Knight to supervise the building of his greenhouses at Sullens Farm in Upminster and to show his son, my cousin, Eric Knight "the ropes", which grandfather did for as long as his help was needed.

My father Ernest Hills had a distinctive turn of colourful phrases, many of which I can still recall. If you'd disagreed with him he would say: "You and I won't talk alike", meaning you were "in for it", and he might even jokingly threaten you with "a fourpenny one" (a punch). To him an old country ignoramus or bumpkin was "a proper wopstraw". If father thought something was unlikely he'd say it would happen "when pussy burns his tail" and if something had gone away to an unspecified place he would say they'd "gone to see Will's mother". I remember that if I ever got into a mess eating a cake which left my face sticky he would say "Don't get yourself barmed all over with that" and if anyone had a bad cough he would say "Nasty bark you got there". I also recall that grandfather Hills had a term of endearment describing someone he was fond of as a little old boy".

Rectory Fields, Corbets Tey Road, Upminster c.1908

In my younger days Mr Cockman and family occupied the last house on the left at the bottom of Howard Road. He was a postman, who also acted as a voluntary groundsman at the cricket club in his spare time. I always remember the boys helping him to move the iron hurdles which enclosed the playing area — these were in place to keep out the various horses which grazed in the Rectory Fields, and also of course the small boys who spent so much time there. Next to Cockman's house was a small green, more a patch of rough grass, on which we sometimes played football. The end fence was made out of railway sleepers, with large spikes (probably platelayers' spikes) placed to make footholds. This formed a short cut for the railmen going to the engine sheds and shunting yards beyond the station on the east side, which could be reached by climbing a small embankment on the other side of the fence.

The Rectory Fields, later the parish Recreation Ground, was the home of several local sporting teams. These included Upminster Thursday football and cricket clubs whose football pitch was just off St Mary's Lane, past the Rectory. They also shared a cricket pitch nearby with Upminster Cricket Club. (The Upminster Football Club - Saturday side - played on a pitch near to and parallel with Corbets Tey Road). The Upminster Thursday teams comprised those who worked in shops and other workplaces for whom Thursday was the early closing day. It was a boy's delight to watch Bob Chester, a notable hitter of boundaries and probably one of the last of the old round-arm bowlers. Bob Chester also played the trumpet and was a member of the small orchestra led by my father which played semi-professionally around the area. Father played a variety of instruments, but most typically he played the violin. Another member that I recall was Lil Aggiss, who played the piano. My grandfather Hills was also a talented musician whose favourite instruments were the concertina and piccolo. My brother John inherited their musical talents, playing the trombone in the Stanford Town Band and also the Band of the 6th Essex Territorial Army.

During term times my spare time in the evenings was mostly taken up with cubs, scouts, the choir, boxing club, and football and cricket in Rectory Fields. On one evening each week I went to cubs, under the Cub Master, the curate Rev. Lewis, assisted by Barbara Wilson, who married the Rector's son, Paul Holden a few years later in 1928. Whereas the scouts spent weekends at camp nearby at Stubbers, where they played on a raft made of old oil drums and planks, we had to be content with just a day there. The age limit for joining the scouts was 12 but we moved out of Upminster before it was time for me to

Upminster St Laurence Cub Pack, mid 1920s

transfer. One member of my cub-pack was Reg Ivey who later became a well-known figure in amateur football, goalkeeper for Met. Police and Hendon F.C. (I believe that he and his younger brother lived at Cranham).

Another evening weekly (Thursdays) was given over to the choir practice at St Laurence church under the direction of Mr Gerald E Sykes, who was also the church organist. Mr Sykes lived in a house on the corner of Cranborne Gardens and he was a solicitor or barrister at Somerset House. He had two daughters, one of whom Betty, who was older than me, later married Jim Kydd, brother of Charlie who served with me in the choir. Mr Sykes was a nice man but he was very strict with the choir. This approach must have been very successful for we had a wonderful choir of a very high standard — all adults had to pass a music sight reading test before they were considered for admission. The repertoire was considerable and they could sing a different setting for Holy Communion every week and a different anthem every Sunday evening. The choir once held a "Café Chantant" at St Laurence Church Hall, the highlight of which was a personal appearance of Ernest Lough, then a choirboy of Temple Church, London who sang "Hear my prayer". He died recently to big write-ups in the national press. Upminster church under the Rev. Holden was

Upminster St Laurence Choirboys, c.1927s. Back row: Payne; Phil Norledge; Ken Kind; Payne; Tony Merchant; Fred Groves; John Hills; Front row: Ernie Halestrap; Peter Hills; Tony Jupp; John Jupp; and Charlie ("Ginger") Kydd.

Upminster St Laurence Choir outing,

"High Church", complete with servers and incense. Before I joined the church choir I was from about the age of six a "boat boy", who carried a receptacle containing incense for the censer held by an adult server at church services. I went on the choirboys' annual outing to Southend, travelling in cars belonging to older choir members. It was a competition to sit in the Rector's car in the "dicky seat" which folded out from the rear boot. When we arrived at Southend the first stop was the boating pool by the pier, then on to the Kursaal, with a ride on the miniature steam railway. After tea at Garon's restaurant near the station, we made our way back to Upminster.

Each Friday evening I went to the Boxing club, which was located in a hut at the end of the footpath from Romford station to Oldchurch Road. After we moved from Upminster I continued boxing firstly as a bantamweight and later a lightweight. One year I won the ABA County Scout Championship at Chelmsford, and during my "career" picked up several other medals which I sadly lost some years ago in a burglary. During the war when on board ship going out to our destination I fought for my battery.

As I've mentioned, our holidays were mostly spent on the farms of relatives but I do recall one occasion soon after the death of my mother when father took us to Great Yarmouth for a week. I remember that we visited the Britannia and Wellington piers to watch the firework displays. We also travelled by steamer to Gorleston, which was a real treat for us.

For indoor pastimes my brother John was kept busy playing with his Meccano set which was added to at Christmas and birthdays. I had a small set but spent much of my time drawing and painting. On Saturday evenings John, my father and I played various board games (snakes and ladders etc.) and card games. On Saturday mornings, however, John and I had to do our weekly jobs, chopping firewood, cleaning knives, boot and shoe cleaning etc. Boots and shoes were repaired at home, until they were too worn. Soles were protected to stop wear by hobnails, which were short nails with a large strong head, while heels and toes were protected by "Blakeys", which was the trade name for shaped metal plates with short nails, sold by sets on cards. As motor traffic was seldom seen in Garbutt Road, we used the roadway to play football with a tennis ball.

Wireless sets were a rarity. I remember my first experience listening to a "cat's whisker" set bought for my Grandmother Hills by my Uncle Jim, in the days before wireless sets with valves. Grandfather Knight had the first wireless set I saw with a horn speaker, exactly as per the trademark of HMV (His Master's Voice). We did have a phonograph, which played records on a cylinder, but by and large it was a placid life by modern standards — no computers, televisions, videos etc — but I am sure a happier one.

Aveley, March 2000

Upminster's Bonanza

June Muncey (née Bolton)

My parents, Sydney and Gladys Bolton née Symes, were married in June 1919 and set up home in Upminster. Before they married they both lived in Leytonstone. Their Upminster home, a semi-detached in Cranham Road (now St Mary's Lane), nearly opposite the Clock House and known as "Cranham House", was a wedding present from Gladys' mother and cost £500. It was recently (1998) sold and fetched in the region of £125,000!

The Bonanza — 42 Station Road — was bought for my mother by my maternal grandmother soon after I was born in June 1920. Mother wanted to run her own business and they sold the house in Cranham Road and moved to the flat above the Bonanza in May 1921, when I was 11 months old. My brother Clifford was born there in July 1925. The Bonanza lived up to its name — it stocked wools, drapery, fancy goods, toys (with the sole local agency for Meccano and Hornby trains until Roomes Stores opened), books, stationery, clocks and watches, Christmas cards etc., etc. There was also a circulating library (2*d* a week), Maids' Registry and a laundry agency! My mother ran the business with the help of Daisy Cudby, who died recently aged over 90. Ivy Wakefield was also with her for many years until the shop was sold in 1939.

Daisy Cudby outside the Bonanza

My father was in the Port of London Authority and he used to catch the 8.15 a.m. train to Fenchurch Street. He would sit in our kitchen having his breakfast while the maid stood at the outside door. When she heard the train coming she would shout out and my father would snatch up his hat and sprint down to the old station and catch it! My father left the PLA to expand the business and we moved to 33 Howard Road in 1929. When we lived at Howard Road father would jump over the back fence and run across the station allotments to catch the train. He hated to waste time waiting for trains and one Christmas I recall that we had to travel in the guard's van to Southend to my grandma's because he had cut things so fine. We were already on the platform begging the guard to wait when father came racing down the stairs and bundled us all into the guard's van. That was one of the rare occasions when my mother was cross! They were childhood sweethearts and I do not know of a happier and more contented couple, nor of kinder or more loving parents. One year they won the "Dunmow Flitch", an event held in Upminster when married couples had to convince the judges that they had not had a cross word for a year and a day! The "flitch" was a side of bacon, and in my parents' case it was truly deserved.

My father's efforts to beat the train were not the only times he displayed his sporting prowess. He was certainly a great sprinter and I remember once when we went to Forest Gate to visit my grandmother and were waiting at the bus stop for the bus to come home when the bus did not stop. My father sprinted after it and reached the next bus stop before it could move off. He put his foot in the door and made it wait until my mother, with my brother in arms, and myself a toddler caught up and were able to climb aboard! My father was a great footballer when he was young and played for West Ham youth team, playing for them at Hampden Park Scotland. He told us (rightly or wrongly) that at school he was known as "the fastest man on the field" .

When I was four years old I first went to school at Upminster College — a grand name for a long wooden hut divided into three classrooms and owned and run by Miss Cooke and her daughter, Miss Cooke junior. This stood in a small grass field where the Capitol Cinema was later built in St Mary's Lane. It was removed to the bottom of Deyncourt Gardens, where it remained for many years until the two Miss Cookes did a "moonlight flit", which caused a great deal of excitement and speculation at the time! In 1927 when I was nearly eight I went to Palmers school at Grays, first as a boarder and then as a day girl, going by train which ran from a siding at the "old" station (the new station was only opened later in the early 1930s).

When I was eight I used to get up at 6 o' clock and go in the milk float with Jack the milkman from Battsons to deliver milk on his first round. There was a large churn at the back of the float with measuring cans hung round it from 2 pint upwards, and the milk was measured into jugs which were left out for us. The early round went down Corbets Tey Road, down Hacton Lane and back round Little Gaynes Lane. The big attraction for me was being allowed to drive the horse. I did this for three or four years and I shall never forget driving along those country lanes in the early morning, in winter with the lamps lit on the front of the float.

When I was a child, one of the highlights of the year was May Day. There was a May Day

St Mary's Lane, prior to redevelopment in the late1920s, with the old Masons Arms on right

procession along the Broadway with our May Queen and her attendants, together with several others from Ockendon, Bulphan, Cranham, Margaretting etc.. They would assemble in the Rector's garden and dance around the maypole. There would be races and teas on the lawn. There was a summer fête in the Rectory Meadows and one day the pig, which was the prize for bowling, escaped and was chased all round the meadows by the cubs and scouts before finally it was caught. In 1925 when I was nearly five I was attendant to the May Queen, Betty Knight.

May Festival procession in Station Road, 1925

We spent most of our leisure time in the Rectory meadows, and enjoyed many picnics there. There was a pond fringed by trees where the bottom of the Rector's garden joined the meadow. A donkey used to graze there. There were ducks on the pond and one hot day, when we were very thirsty, we drank some of the muddy water, with no apparent ill effects. My father was on the Parish Council and was instrumental in having the tennis courts made after the meadows were acquired as a recreation ground. The cricket pavilion was a converted railway carriage.

When we moved to Howard Road what had been the lounge upstairs above the shop became a showroom. I remember the fireworks being displayed on a long trestle table which ran the length of the room - everyone came to the Bonanza for their fireworks. Christmas too was a very busy time and the shop would be open until 9 p.m. or later on Christmas Eve. The highlight to me was having our hot lunch brought along to us by Frizzell the baker, covered with a cotton cloth. Lighting was supplied by gas and it was a memorable day when we had electricity connected at the Bonanza. Eventually, probably in the late 1920s, we had an electric train running round the larger of the Bonanza's two front windows.

At this time we also had a large showcase on the pavement in front of the shop – the fore-court was very much wider then. When Roomes Stores opened in 1927, followed by the Depression, it became an increasingly difficult struggle to carry on a successful business. We gave up the house in Howard Road and moved back to above the shop in 1932. We were very cramped, as several of the rooms were still used as stockrooms and showrooms and there was an extra one of us now, as my sister Hazel was born at Howard Road in July 1932, shortly before we moved back. With my parents paying school fees for me at Palmers School in Grays my father tried many different ways of augmenting our income, including cycling for miles around Upminster and Grays selling children's encyclopae-dias; travelling as a representative for ladders; and buying old bicycles on Romford market, painting them and selling them. I know of at least two people who had one of these old bicycles for over thirty years!

To me the Bonanza was Upminster and I could not imagine the "village" existing without it! Eventually in 1939 the Bonanza was sold to Hilberry Chaplin, the Estate Agent, and we moved down to Cambridge near relatives.

My father had served in France during the 1914-18 war, initially with the 7th City of London Battalion, and he was eventually promoted to lieutenant in the Royal Engineers. At the end of the war he was placed on the Officers' Emergency Reserve. He was a founder member of the British Legion after the first war when it opened in Cranham. Shortly after the outbreak of war in 1939 he was called up and promoted to captain with the Royal Engineers. He was stationed in this country, firstly in Hampshire, then in Stranraer and finally at the War Office until 1946. My parents had bought a large house in a village near Cambridge during the war and this was filled with various members of the family and friends who came down at weekends and for longer periods to escape the blitz. My mother was wonderful and really "kept the home fires burning" during those difficult years when father was away from home.

BOOKS *to interest children of all ages.*

Children's minds are as hungry as their bodies. They are as eager to devour a book full of pictures as to eat their dinner. And just as you build up their bodies on wholesome food, so you will build up their minds by giving them the best the printed page can offer.

The Bonanza has a wonderful selection of healthy literature, books full of the best and brightest stories to appeal to all boys and girls.

Trimmed and Furnished Folding Cots.

i. DOLLS

With and without Hair.

Dressed

6d. to 25/-

DOLLS

Mama.

Unbreakable

6d. to 25/-

Dolly's very own bed.
This folding cot is a source of joy to all little girls.
Trimmed with dainty materials, it has a mattress and white enamel frame, each being packed in a box.

To take dolls up to	11 ins.	15 ins.	17 ins.	21 ins.	24 ins.	28 ins.
	7/11	8/11	9/11	10/11	15/11	21/-

Trimmed and furnished with mattress, pillow, pair of blankets, pair of sheets and frilled quilt.

To take dolls up to	11 ins.	15 ins.	17 ins,	21 ins.	24 ins.	28 ins.
	12/11	13/11	15/11	21/-	25/11	32/6

Meccano

3/6 to

£18-5-0

Spare parts
in stock

Hornby
Trains

6/- to

£5-10-0

Spare parts
in stock

Meccano is real Engineering in miniature. All the parts are exact replicas of those used in real engineering practice and can be used to make hundreds of different working models. Meccano is the greatest gift a boy can have!

Toys Showroom. First Floor.

The BONANZA - "The Treasure Chest" - **Upminster**

Extract from Bonanza sales advertisement, late 1920s

After my father was demobbed in 1946 he sat for an examination for a post in the Civil Service, placing ninth out of over 500 applicants. He became a Planning Officer in the Ministry of Works, Cambridge, until he retired in 1962. My father died in Ipswich, Suffolk in 1982, aged nearly 86, as the result of a tragic road accident when a drunken driver hit him and my mother. My mother, who was badly injured, survived until 1988, when she died at the age of 91.

Anniversary of Sydney and Gladys in June 1944. Standing: June, Clifford and Hazel. Seated: Sydney and Gladys

The shops I can remember in Station Road, or the Broadway as it was then in 1920, were on the left from the Station to the Bell Hotel: Pudneys the greengrocer; Victoria wine; Frizzells, the baker; the Chemist (Humphreys I think); Tolworthy, the butcher; and Greens stores, (also a Post Office for a while). After Howard Road came: Goodchilds, the drapers; Copleys the ironmonger (a legend!); International Stores; Davis, the gentlemen's outfitters; Miss Patrick, a little home-made cake shop; Reeves the hardware store; the Bonanza; a sweet shop; an Estate agents; Searson's the shoe shop; Talbots the greengrocer; Anglins fish shop; Miss Leeney, the sweet shop; and Watkins the barber, on the corner. Tolworthy the butcher made all his deliveries with pony and trap and there was a great commotion one day when one of his ponies slipped over on the icy road outside his shop. It had to be taken out of the trap before they could get it to its feet again.

After St Lawrence Road was: Battsons the dairy; Dales paper shop; Talbots garage; and the Boys' School. After the school was another row of little shops, one of which was Frizzells the baker, an Estate Agent (I think) and Jupps the butchers. Then, jutting out in front of them all, was the legendary Cosy Corner and on the opposite corner of Corbets Tey Road, the magnificent Bell Hotel.

On the other side of Station Road was the Crumpled Horn Diary, then I think Kemp's the Chemist, an opticians and, on the corner of Branfill Road, Dr Bletsoe, our much-loved Doctor. I believe it cost us 2s 6d to visit him and 5s if he came to us. In the early 1930s someone had the brilliant idea of erecting a large circular, heavy canvas swimming pool in the yard of the men's club behind Dr Bletsoe's house. This was very popular but, unfortunately, one day it burst and the water — gallons of it — poured down into the back of Dr Bletsoe's house and rushed out the front door! It was not re-erected! We heard later that it did not burst but was punctured by airgun pellets fired by a lad whose house faced the pool and whose family was fed up with the noise. Needless to say, this was never proved.

Station Road in the1930s - the Bonanza's glass display case can be seen on the pavement outside the shop to the right of the photo.

Station Road looking towards the station, in the 1920s, with Dr Bletsoe's house and surgery on the far left

On the opposite corner of Branfill Road was a bank (I think the Westminster) then fields until Roomes was built, then a ladies hairdresser and Lush and Cooke, the dry cleaners. I think there was another bank on the corner of Gaynes Road (after the Congregational Church) and then the Girls' School. The nearest shop I can remember was Cant, the cobbler, followed by Abraham, the baker — a cottage shop with a long front garden with the bakery behind and then his yard and stables. Abrahams shop was the most typical village bakery you could imagine and the Abrahams were the most wonderful people. The baker himself had endless time and patience to allow me and my little friends to have a piece of dough, make a little loaf, and put it into his long oven with the wooden spatulas with the long handles, then to watch him take it out and give it to us to eat when baked. At Christmas we took our turkey to Mr Abraham to be cooked, with many others, in his bread oven. We used to buy a pennyworth of sweets from his little shop on a Saturday, taking ages to choose from the different jars, and then sit in a row on his wall and eat them. What things the children of today miss! Every Good Friday morning before breakfast we had two dozen hot-cross buns delivered — one dozen from Abrahams and one dozen from Frizzells — and we could never remember from one year to the next which ones were better.

Sometimes in the early 1930s on Saturday mornings my brother Clifford and I would go to the windmill. Mr Abraham, the miller who was related to Mr Abraham the baker, would take us to the top of the windmill, and from the little platform outside we could see the Crystal Palace.

There was a little stall selling vegetables after Abrahams, then Aggiss' garage. Their chestnut tree on the corner of their forecourt was magnificent and there was a great outcry and numerous protests, all to no avail of course, when it was felled for development. There was an alleyway past Aggiss' with another Green's stores on the corner, and a small draper's shop next to it. After that it was all private houses along the Hornchurch Road.

Down Corbets Tey Road past the Bell it was all houses and cottages opposite the Rectory Meadow. Immediately past the Bell were several very large houses, followed by a row of country cottages with very long front gardens. There was another large house where a girl called "Bluebell" Abney lived with her little brother, then came a farm (which I believe was Hunts) with a high brick wall along the Corbets Tey Road as far, I think, as the turning left into the new Springfield estate. Opposite was a farm (Hoppey Hall) with a lovely cedar tree in the front and we delivered milk there. This is now a garage and a large car park. There were then fields and houses right up to the forge at Corbets Tey. I was often taken up there to see the horses shod and I shall never forget the acrid smell of the red-hot shoes when they were put on the horse's hoof! At the bottom of Corbets Tey Road turning right was (and still is) a very large house called Harwood Hall. We used to canter up the long drive to deliver milk and I remember the beautiful crocus flowers there in the spring.

Down Hacton Lane, on the right before Park Corner Farm was a pair of small farm cottages, two-up, two-down, where a farm labourer and his wife named Letch lived. We stopped there on our milk round every morning about 6.30 a.m. for a cup of tea with lots of sugar. It was a tiny living room, mostly taken up with a large table and kitchen range, with a low ceiling festooned with sticky fly papers: I was fascinated by the flies that wriggled and often fell off from these crowded traps. It was lovely and warm in the winter and we warmed our hands round the mugs of hot, sweet tea. They must have been very poor but Mrs Letch was so kind. I often wish I could have met her in later years, but the cottage has long gone.

Harwood Hall - one of the places where June Bolton used to deliver milk in the 1920s.

I remember the Arterial road to Southend being built and opened and, after the ceremony, my little friends and I tentatively took a few steps on it and all agreed that it felt quite different to walk on!

When Howard Road was extended and new bungalows built in about 1930, they cost £375. Some of the larger houses in Corbets Tey Road cost nearly £1,000 which we thought was phenomenal. When the first Roomes Stores was built in 1927 I watched the progress from our living room windows upstairs. A night watchman had a brazier and a little hut in the road outside; I was very sorry when he went as I loved to see his fire glowing in the dark.

In about 1925 our first car was an old "tin Lizzie" Ford and my three little friends, whose father had a lovely Chrysler which he garaged at Talbots, thought ours was infinitely superior. My father had to crank it with a starting handle (which sprang back and sprained his wrist) and it would only go up hills in reverse.

In the early 1920s a little band of ex-servicemen used to walk down the Broadway singing and playing musical instruments. My father always gave very generously to them and I always wanted to cry. In the General Strike men used to climb into lorries in the Broadway near the station, to get to London.

Trains ran on Christmas Day then and in the 1930s we used to go early on Christmas morning by Green Line Coach to Liverpool Street and catch the train to Whittlesford, Cambridgeshire, and arrive in time for Christmas lunch. We could not go on Christmas Eve because the shop was open so late. Post, too, was delivered on Christmas morning. Postmen wore uniforms and peaked caps — so did railway porters and bus drivers. Men wore bowler hats, starched wing collars and spats to work in the City. When we were at school we always had to wear our hats and boys their caps and we always knew where to find a policeman — at the Bell Corner!

Coventry, February 2000

Policeman on duty outside the Chestnuts Garage, at the Bell Corner, late 1920s

Tadlows and other memories

Joan Hills

I was born at 14 Garbutt Road, Upminster on 21 April 1922, the fourth child of Ernest Jonathan Hills and Edith. My mother, who was the daughter of Walter and Annie Knight of Park Corner Farm, Hacton, died of puerperal sepsis just eight days after my birth, aged 34. What a waste of a young life: in these days of antibiotics, women no longer die of that.

My father, finding himself a widower at 32 with three small children, unfortunately became embittered by his wife's death. Theirs had been a very short married life - not quite eight years, almost half of which my father spent in the army during the First World War. After the birth of two sons, my brothers John and Peter, two years apart, they must have hoped for a daughter. She was duly born on 10 June 1920 at Park Corner Farm — my sister Betty Margaret — but sadly she only lived a month. I do not know at what point they moved from Park Corner Farm to their own home in Garbutt Road, but their married life together there must have been less than two years, culminating in my mother's death on 29 April 1922. And the rest, as they say, is history.

Wedding of Ernest Hills and Edith Knight, May 1914: Standing (Left to right) Aunt May Knight; Grandfather Jonathan Hills; Herbert Edwards (best man); father Ernest Hills; mother Edith Knight; Grandfather Walter John (Jack) Knight; Aunt Emma (Bet) Knight. Seated (left to right): Aunt Helen Hills; Grandmother Eliza Hills née Sparrow, with Evelyn Sparrow (cousin); Grandmother Annie Knight (née Taylor) with cousins Jack Knight junior and Grace Knight.

Both my brother Peter and I are interested in family history, and Peter was fortunate enough to be given copies of quite a few funeral accounts of members of both the Hills and Knight families. Among the accounts is the one for my mother's funeral and from this I know who dug her grave (Old Bill Huckle) and who the bearers were (Messrs George, Enever, Coe and Dines). I do not feel in the least morbid about this, in fact it is a rather comfortable link with my roots.

With my mother's death a whole new surrogate family came into my life. Our neighbours at 12 Garbutt Road were an elderly couple called Bill and Kate Hammond, who had four children (Will, Louie, Annie and George) of very similar age to my father and his brothers. Nan and Grandad, as I still call them, were not related to us at all. Their son Will worked for my maternal Grandad Knight and so Nan and Grandad already knew my mother, of whom they were very fond. One of the few things my father told me was that when mother realised that she was dying she asked Nan if she would take me, saying (according to my father) "Daddy can look after the boys if Nanny will have my baby!" This she duly did and looked after me for the first five years of my life. I remember those first years very clearly in some respects, in particular that I would run to meet Grandad Hammond when he came home from work and be hoisted up on his shoulders. He was a horseman and, in his working corduroys, smelled strongly of horse. On Sunday, scrubbed and ready to go to the little chapel in St Lawrence Road, he smelled of Erasmic Shaving Soap. Nan died of cancer at the beginning of the war and Grandad remained at no.12, I believe, until his death. Mr Nunn who lived next door at no. 10 (and conducted Grandad's funeral at Corbets Tey) told me that during the air raids the old gentleman would stand in the garden with the lights on. One night Mr Nunn went out to remonstrate with him and Grandad said "Are they h'ourn, Bert?" to which Bert Nunn replied: "No Bill, they h'ain't h'ourn they's Huns. You git in that house." Unfortunately there's no way of reproducing the accent! Bert and Grandad said "house" in a way which does not come across on paper. Grandad called some houses in St Mary's Lane "Mis' Mansfield's hausen" — almost a pure Anglo-Saxon plural, I've been told. She was "Mrs." which he pronounced quickly as "Mis'" and not "Missus".

My father Ernest Hills was born at Goldings Cottages, Great Warley on 21 November 1889. He was the eldest son of Jonathan Hills, who became the head gardener to Mr Henry Joslin at Gaynes Park around 1892, and his wife Eliza née Sparrow. Grandfather Jonathan was born in Great Warley on 6 February 1857 and I think the family later moved to Tyler's Hall Farm, Upminster Common when his father James was promoted from being an agricultural labourer to farm bailiff for Mr Lescher. Great grandad died of facial cancer in August 1875 and my father could go into gruesome details about this. As this took place 14 years before Dad was born I assume he had heard about this either from his father or two aunties, grandad's older sisters, Ellen and Emma, one single and one a widow who lived in Goldings Cottages, both dying in 1930. Father also told me that the priest rode out on horseback from Brentwood RC church (it was then St Helen's, long before it became the cathedral) to give great grandad the Last Rites.

My grandparents moved to Tadlows (now 251 Corbets Tey Road) when grandfather started at Gaynes and so my father came to Upminster when he was three or a little older. Dad told me that the day of their move from Great Warley to Upminster was a wet one and some of the move was done by pony and trap. He remembered sitting down under the waterproof "apron" at his mother's feet and hearing the rain drumming above him. Tadlows was then divided into two houses and the Hills family lived in the left-hand side as you look at the house from the road. They had two rooms downstairs, two bedrooms above that, and a large attic room. What a family! My grandparents had five boys in just under six years and then a gap of six years before the birth of the only girl. My father, who was the oldest, had the little back bedroom to himself while the other four boys — Jim, Bob, Tom and Harry — shared two double beds up in the attic room. I expect that my father lost his own room when auntie Helen (born 1901), six years younger than the youngest of the boys, became too old to sleep in the front bedroom with her parents. There was no inside toilet, and the W.C. was still down the bottom of the garden when I remember it in the 1930s, although by then a flush toilet had been installed.

Tadlows, now 251 Corbets Tey Road .

A few summers ago I plucked up the courage to knock at the front door of Tadlows and introduce myself. I was very courteously received by Mrs Glenys Wylde, who lived there and was pleased to show me the house, now back as one dwelling. I told her quite a bit about my family and sent her some photos. It was strange to stand in the hall and turn left into the front room, through a doorway which had been bricked in when my grandfather lived there. I was intrigued to see the kitchens on either side of the house now made into one large room. I was able to show Mrs Wylde where the temporary stairs had gone up on our side of the house. She also showed me the beautiful inglenook fireplace which had been uncovered in the right hand front room.

My father had a fund of stories about his childhood at Tadlows. When he and his brothers were all small boys, someone hanged himself in one of the cottages at the back of Tadlows. Boys will be boys and when the policeman arrived to cut the body down the five brothers all crowded round the door. All very interesting — until the breath left the body with a groan, and five small boys fled for home as fast as their legs would carry them!

A still rural Corbets Tey Road in the late 1920s

Old Jinny German lived in the first row of cottages in Corbets Tey Road, which had the old loos at the bottom of the garden (called in Essex at least, The Bumby hole). The Hills boys would wait for Old Jinny to go down to the bottom of the garden, open the door at the back of the loo, normally used for removing the bucket, and tickle the old lady's bare backside with a long feather. They were also known to put fireworks down cottage chimneys!

On one occasion Granny sent the youngest two Hills boys, Tom and Harry, into Upminster with the go-cart (a wooden box on wheels) to fetch some sugar. They took turns in pushing it the mile home. When one brother got to Gaynes Lodge opposite Little Gaynes Lane he said to the other brother "Your turn now", to which the other replied "We're almost home, you can take it the rest of the way". Two obstinate Hillses, neither would give in, so they left the sugar where it was and went home. On hearing what they had done Gran clouted two backsides and sent them back. Surprise, surprise the sugar had gone, and Tom and Harry spent the night in someone's barn until the parental wrath had worn off.

Gaynes Cross, Corbets Tey Road with Gaynes Lodge on the left and the junction with Little Gaynes Lane and the entrance to Gaynes Park on the right.

My father's last few working years before his retirement in 1954 were spent at Ardale School, North Stifford where he was Headmaster's Clerk. Ardale was an approved school for teenage delinquent boys and one day Dad came home and said to my stepmother "You know, Mary, if there had been such a thing as Ardale in our school days, all five of us would have been in it." However, I don't agree that the brothers' pranks would have landed them in that sort of trouble: my grandfather had a "short fuse" and a strap on the back of the kitchen door! I gather he was a very strict father, but very loving grandfather to us. His pet name for me was "Polly" and my appearance round the kitchen door was greeted with "Well, Polly". In contrast, I remember Granny Hills as a rather rigid lady. It was a penance to go and stay at Tadlows because she would sit me on the potty in the kitchen long after I considered it was dignified!

Auntie Helen told me how Granny Hills had said that when the boys were small, she would get them ready from the oldest (my father) downwards and as each one was ready he would be tied to a leg of a sturdy, plain mahogany table while she got the baby, Uncle Harry, ready. It was the only way she went out with five clean sons! When Helen died in 1983 my brother Peter, who was her executor, asked me if I would like anything from her flat. I said "Yes, please, her drop-leaf table" — the very same piece of furniture to which my father and his brothers had been secured. I still have that table which I call the "Tadlows Table". One of my hobbies is dolls' houses and one of mine, not unlike Tadlows (except that it has an extra storey) with its own nameplate, custom-made for me, stands on Tadlows Table. It is a grand old piece of cottage furniture that shows signs of much use. At one time I got a quote to have it re-polished, changing my mind when I realised the cost. The rather precise gentleman who gave me a quote told me it dated back much further than my grandparents' wedding in 1889, probably to the early years of the nineteenth century.

Grandfather Jonathan Hills of Tadlows

My father and all the Hills family attended the village school and the five boys all became choirboys at St Laurence Church. This tradition continued, as my father and my two older brothers John and Peter were all later members of the choir. Father and three of his brothers all served in France in the First World War. Dad was a signaller in the Middlesex Regiment, Jim a gunner in the Royal Field Artillery, Tom in the Royal Army Medical Corps, and Harry served in the Dragoon Guards. Sadly Tom lost his life in September 1916 and his name is recorded on Upminster's war memorial. Tom always comes across to me as a bit of an "odd bod", but someone with a great feel for animals and people. He was in the habit of bringing home wounded birds and animals, and once produced a very large grass snake from the inside of his jacket — at which my grandmother passed out cold! On his death the newspaper report quotes grandmother as saying of her son "If any kindness was needed, especially to old people, he was the one to do it." My favourite family story about him is when he went to visit a very old man, Reuben Butt, in the cottages at the back of Tadlows. Reuben had been admitted to Oldchurch Hospital, then the Workhouse Infirmary, but wouldn't stay. Tom went to see him at home and asked "Why wouldn't you stay, Reuben? Weren't they kind to you?" Reuben replied in the high piping voice of a very old man: "It were all right Tom, but a li'l slip of a girl came along and put me in a bath, and it were that hot, and I said to her 'Hey, what you think you're a doin' of, Miss, scaldin' a pig?'" I think it was probably the only time in his life that Reuben had been in a bath!

Tom received his fatal wounds during an act of bravery for which he was posthumously awarded the Military Medal. Serving in France with the RAMC on 9 September 1916 he had already brought in one wounded man and, in an attempt to fetch in another, he was seriously wounded when a shell burst close to him. He was sent back to the Netley Military Hospital, Southampton from where he was able to write home to his parents. The next day my grandparents received a letter telling them that he was now dangerously ill. They hastened to Southampton but he passed away before they could reach the hospital. His body was brought back to Upminster where he was buried at Corbets Tey after a well-attended funeral service at St Laurence Church. Subsequently buried there with Tom have been his parents, Aunt Amelia Sparrow (Granny's aunt) and Auntie Helen's ashes.

Some six months earlier in March 1916 a letter from my uncle Harry (Tom and dad's brother), of which I have a copy, was published in the *Romford Recorder*. This gives a far from jingoistic account about the horrors of life in the trenches, with graphic descriptions of fellow soldiers' deaths and reference to a "sight fit for nobody to see", the bodies of at least 300 dead lying along the wire. At first I thought that this letter must have been written to Harry's only sister, Helen, but in view of the fact that the wording of the letter refers to "the guv'nor, mother and little Mic" (the latter being Helen's pet name) I think it really must have been written to my mother, as Uncle Harry was very fond of her. My father told me how, on one occasion when Harry was on leave, he took mother up to Barker's in Oxford Street to buy a new coat. Uncle Harry was in uniform and mother left John, then about a year old, with him while she went off to try on coats. She came back to find a red-faced crying baby, and a red-faced Guardsman, surrounded by shop girls! As Uncle Harry was very shy, he must have been very fond of his sister-in-law to take her on a shopping expedition.

A studio portrait of Tom Hills, in his Royal Army Medical Corps uniform

My Grandad Hills lived at Tadlows until his death in 1939. I think it's possible that this may have helped to save Tadlows from the fate of all the other big houses on Corbets Tey Road. I know that Colonel Sir Francis Whitmore of Orsett Hall left a clause in his will that all the old estate employees, and their widows after them, should be allowed to live out their lives in their tied housing and I've wondered whether Mr Joslin made a similar provision. Certainly, grandfather continued to live there when he retired after his employer Joslin's death in 1927. In contrast his daughter, my Auntie Helen, had to vacate Tadlows when her father died. Tadlows was offered to my father for £300 but he could not have raised that sort of money at the time and, in any event, his second wife (my step-mother) was against the idea. In view of the expense of what would have been involved in the upkeep of Tadlows, now a grade two listed building, things probably turned out for the best.

When Grandad Jonathan Hills died in January 1939 a lengthy and quite flattering obituary appeared in the local press: I think I detect my father's hand in this! As well as sketching in grandad's upbringing and career as a gardener before coming to Gaynes in 1892, it gives details about his interests and character. He was said to be an excellent sportsman, chiefly at cricket, a crack shot "with rifle, revolver and gun" and a "devotee of music playing most instruments ... the piccolo and violin being his favourites." The obituary went on to record that "his personality made him loved and understood by all wild creatures, his control of bird and beast being almost uncanny". It was claimed that as a keen local historian he had supplied Upminster's chronicler Thomas Wilson "with much data for his book *The story of Upminster*" although as Wilson's book came out in 1881, some 11 years before grandfather came to Upminster, I think this is highly unlikely. In any case, grandfather did not come from Upminster but Great Warley.

Children of Walter John Knight and Annie Emma née Taylor c.1905: Standing: Edith and Walter John (known as Jack). Seated: Emma (known as Bet) and May

My mother Edith Annie Knight (known as Edie) was born in December 1887. She had two brothers, one older (Jack) and one younger (Joe), and two sisters, both younger. Jack, Edie and Joe were born in Aveley and after my grandparents moved to Hacton two more girls were born, Emma (always called Bet) born in 1892 and May, born 1895, who was my godmother. Aunt May, like my father's only sister Helen, remained single. Jack (who I believe was Walter John, after his father) married Annie Aggiss in 1909 and they had two sons, my cousins "young" Jack, and Eric. Mother's younger brother Joseph (Joe), two years her junior, died in July 1897 at the age of seven. He had a heart condition which is a consequence of rheumatic fever and died of pneumonia. Because of family likeness I am fairly sure that he is the little boy on the front row of mother's school group, a poorly child with spindly legs like match sticks. I think that the photo was probably taken in the summer of 1897, just before he died. The Knight family came to Upminster before 1892 and mother attended the Upminster Girls' and Infants School in Station Road. Because of the distance from her home at Hacton, a good two miles, she was allowed to bring her bicycle to school, the only child permitted to do so.

My maternal grandfather Walter Knight was 65 when he died at Park Corner Farm on 12 March 1928 and the family connection with the farm came to an end, a Mr Mann, I

Upminster Girls' and Infants' school c.1897. Edith Knight is on the right, with bicycle which she was allowed to bring to school because of the distance from her home. The solitary boy in the front row is thought to be her brother, Joe Knight, who died soon after

believe, taking over the land after this. I was not quite six when he died but I can still remember a fair bit about the interior of the house. I can hear in my imagination the sound of the pump over the old stone sink in the big kitchen. I did not like going past the steps, which led from the passage going across the house down to the cellar, where the knife-grinding machine was kept, and also where the shoes were cleaned. I remember the main staircase with a copper warming pan hanging on the wall as you looked up the stairs; the stairs then turned right, and right again onto the main landing. Before this was a smaller landing and from this opened a little bedroom which had to be entered through what was either another small room, or a large cupboard with no windows. This was another source of terror to me, and I would take a deep breath and scoot past as fast as my little legs would carry me. I don't remember much more about upstairs, except that there was a large wooden chest on the main landing. Downstairs I can visualise the drawing room with a window seat and deep armchairs covered in a light chintz patterned with big sprays of lilac. There was a beautiful Welsh dresser with a clock, which you saw against the left-hand wall as you opened the door from the passage. There was a very large oil lamp over the kitchen table which must have been weighted in some way, because it could be pulled down to provide a good light over the table or given a push to go up to the ceiling again. Aunt Bet told me that the three Knight sisters used to sit round the table and sew by the light of this oil lamp. The two younger girls embroidered mother's wedding veil as their wedding present to her. This was left spread out on one of the spare beds and was never folded up until it was finished. I had it until quite recently and now my brother's daughter, Mary, has it. Mary also has mother's trousseau nightdress: high neck, blue ribbon threaded through eyelet holes, blue butterflies embroidered down the front and long sleeves finished with lace frill. One could wear it at a fancy dress party — and feel overdressed.

Mother Edith Knight (seated) and her sister, Aunt Bet Knight.

I surprised Aunt Bet one day by telling her how much I remembered about the farm. The ceiling of the passage which led straight through the house from the front door to the back changed levels, reflecting the step in the landing above. On the "upright" of this change of level was a stuffed canary in a glass case with a butterfly beside him. When I told Aunt Bet about this she said "Good gracious, fancy you remembering that - that was Pip, my canary."

Some of the small things that my father said about the farm come to mind. If anyone in the family was out at night they would tap on the kitchen window to be let in, whereupon my grandmother would throw open the door. But it wasn't always a person who walked in but the two house cats, Smut and Monkey, at which Nanny Knight would exclaim "Oh you ...".

My mother and Aunt Bet were courting at the same time. My grandfather kept some cows and it was the girls' job to churn the butter. Apparently, in certain weather conditions, the butter is slow to "come" and on these occasions my father and uncle Bert (Herbert Thorogood - who married Aunt Bet in 1915) would be waiting impatiently down the lane for their dates, no doubt guessing why the girls were so late.

I can remember what I gave Nan and Grandad Hammond every Christmas: a new "modest vest" for her and a new red and white patterned cotton handkerchief for him. He always took the heel of a loaf and a big piece of cheese to work with him tied up in a big red and white handkerchief. Grandad Hammond originally worked for Jack Joslin at Hunts and I liked to go down and "help" him bring in his horses, Derby and Boxer, at the end of the working day. I would walk too close to the lead horse and the old gentleman would say, with the rising East Anglian inflection: "You mind she don't treed on yer". "She" probably wouldn't have known my feet were there!

After Hunts Farm and its land were sold in the 1930s, he went to work with his son Will at Park Corner Farm. Grandad was then in his 70s and walked each day from Garbutt Road to Hacton and back again at night. Within the last fifteen years I met up with grandad's oldest grandson, Charlie Slocombe, whose mother Louie lived in one of the Post Office Cottages in Corbets Tey Road. Charlie told me that when he got his first motorbike he went to meet grandad from work and offered him a lift home. The old gentleman preferred to trudge on, eyeing the motor bike with some distrust! His daughter Louie had been married to Charlie Slocombe, a soldier who had been killed in the First World War when serving with the Duke of Cornwall's Light Infantry. Louie had continued to receive letters from her husband long after she had heard that he had been killed. She was left to bring up Charlie junior and younger brother George on her own. In the 1920s or 30s she developed one of the distressing neurological conditions which caused her to develop a tremor and her tongue became too big for her mouth. The old people said it was brought on by shock.

Louie's next-door neighbour Mrs Hope had a lodger, David Cruickshank, who was an engine driver and had a daughter Rosie, who was about my age. Her mother too had died when she was born. She and I used to play together with Judy Abney, who lived in one of the end cottages that had an extra upper storey.

On 3 July 1927 my father married again. My stepmother was Mary Elizabeth Claxton who

Post Office Cottages, Corbets Tey Road. These cottages were demolished in the late 1930s

St Laurence parish church.

had come to father as housekeeper and stayed on to become his wife. They were married in St Laurence Church in July 1927, less than a year before work on the church extension began. We knew that Auntie Mary, as we called her, was older than my father but it was not until her death on Boxing Day 1960 that we found out that she was 13 years older than him, so he was 37 and she was 50 when they married. I'm sure she deliberately kept the age difference a secret. On their wedding lines she is shown as eight years his senior but she had actually been born in August 1876. When the pensions people came to interview them before Dad became of pensionable age they tried to pin her down as to her actual date of birth, at which she became "shirty" and claimed to have been born before the days of compulsory registration of births (which of course was nonsense). She was tiny — I doubt that she was even five feet tall — and weighed about six stone, so she could easily carry off losing a few years.

We were all very glad when she married father. I wish I could say that she was equally glad. On one occasion she said to me "I married your father for the sake of you three children." I have often thought since "What courage!", for my father was a far from easy person. I am sure that we all loved her dearly, in fact my brother Peter's daughter was named for her: Mary Elizabeth.

By coincidence both my natural mother and stepmother were seamstresses, and so Auntie Mary made both her own wedding dress and my bridesmaids dress. Her dress was a very pale fawn material with a silvery sheen, while mine was an apricot silk, smocked on the shoulders and at the waist, with two little ties at the neck, each ending in a tassel. I had a white straw hat with ruched ribbon under the brim, and in fact I have a snap of myself wearing it, taken on the Rectory Meadow. I also wore white socks with an openwork pattern, always called by my brother's "Kate's caterpillar socks", Kate being their childhood name for me. Aunt May, who was a great knitter, kept me supplied in socks of this pattern — white for best, and fawn for school. We both carried rosebuds, which were sent up from Portsmouth, in the days when parcels were delivered in one day, by Auntie Mary's sister Eliza, who we always called Auntie Li. Nanny Hammond would not let Auntie Mary prepare any vegetables that week, so that she had nice, unstained hands to present when it came to my father putting the ring on her third finger.

I'm sure that Aunt Mary's family was related in some way to the Abraham family who owned the windmill — possibly through her mother whose family were bakers. One of Auntie Mary's brothers had the second name Clement, which was the name of one of the Abraham brothers who were the millers, and another brother had Abraham for a second name. She used to refer to the old gentleman in charge of the mill as Uncle John.

One of the things that contributed to make my father a difficult man was the fact that, in modern jargon, he never reached his full potential. Like his father, my dad was very musical but was unable to fulfil this as a career. Before going into the Army in World War One he was a grocer's assistant, firstly at Gooderham's in Upminster and then, after he and my mother married in May 1914, he got a job in Enfield. My eldest brother John was born in February 1915 and dad would not go into the Army until John was safely born. After the war like so many ex-servicemen he had difficulty finding work. On my sister's death certificate in July 1920 his occupation was stated as "railway carriage cleaner - ex-Army", which says it all. Finally he got a job as a storekeeper at the London Thames Haven Oil Wharves near Stanford le Hope, which is why we moved to Grays in 1929. For reasons best known to himself he went back into the

Ernest Hills, with hands on hips, outside Kemps Grocers Store, probably at Southend c.1912.

Army in World War Two, aged 51, and on demobilisation did a variety of clerical jobs, culminating in being headmaster's clerk at Ardale School. This was a job he thoroughly enjoyed because, in addition to his clerical duties, he formed a small band which appears to have been quite a success with the boys.

I probably get the "gift of the gab" from my father, who was a great one for reminiscing. He would start to talk about a lot of the old people in the village and it would be "And there was old Mr. So-and-so — he's dead and gone. And I remember old Mrs So-and-so — she's dead and gone!" Auntie Mary would stand behind Dad and look at us over his shoulder, mouthing the words "And he's dead and gone", making it difficult for us to keep a straight face. Dad could take you, in imagination, on a "guided tour" of the churchyard and tell a tale, not always respectful, of most people buried there.

The sound of the wind in trees is still very evocative for me. I wonder if anyone else remembers the elm trees along the bottoms of the gardens in Garbutt Road? The rooks always built in these trees, and Nan said that if she wanted to keep me quiet she would put me in my cradle in the kitchen window where I could see and hear the birds and the sound of the trees. This sound also reminds me of walking down Corbets Tey Road to Tadlows. In those days, of course, the houses in Garbutt Road had sash windows, and the top window was always down in hot weather. I had a crocheted white woollen doll with embroidered features and a tuft of ginger wool for hair. My brothers John and Peter would station themselves — one in the garden and one in the kitchen — and throw Ginger to one another through the open window to a chorus of "Look, auntie, Ginger's flying".

I have many memories of St Laurence Church. I think Dad and the boys must have gone to 9.30 a.m. Sung Eucharist, but certainly Auntie Mary and possibly my father went to 11 o'clock Matins. There was Sunday School in the Church Hall and then the children were brought back into the church for the latter part of the service, during which we were allowed to "kneel up" on our hassocks, turn round and draw a picture of what we had learnt in Sunday School. For many years Auntie Mary kept my picture of Palm Sunday, with palms up in the sky as well as on the road. This was kept in a box with some of my "corkscrew" curls, and I think both were thrown out when someone told her it was unlucky to keep a child's hair. I have St Laurence to thank for my abiding love of church music. Mr Gerald Sykes was organist and choirmaster and was responsible for the very high standard to be found at that time. I also remember watching the man pumping the organ — I think he was somewhere over to the left of the high altar. This was, of course,

Upminster St Laurence Church Choir: June 1929. Back Row: Mr Charles Jupp junior; M B Roome; William Key; P Nunn; Paul Holden; Ernest ("Tiny") Gates; Mr Leonard Jupp senior; Gerald Sykes, choir master; Mr Walter Wallace; Frank Norledge; Ernest Hills; Edmund ("Ted") Pearmain; Messrs Taylor, Jarvis, and Hepplewhite. Second Row: Mr Newton, church warden; Mrs Marian Gates; Mrs Mowat; Mrs Mary Ann Sorrell; Mrs Tyler; Miss Gillings; Miss Kydd; Miss Symes; Miss Kydd; Miss Coverley; Miss Noakes; Miss Sheidow; Miss Youngs; Miss Nunn; Miss Hepplewhite; Miss Holden; Miss Taylor; Miss Compton; Mr Littlejohn. Seated: Miss Thear; Mrs Boyd; Mrs Maude Jupp; Miss Edwards; Miss Ginbey; Miss Violet Jupp; Rev H H Holden; Miss Hilda Halestrap; Miss Turner; Miss ?; Miss Fidgen; Mrs Cable; and Miss Gibbs. Choirboys seated on floor: Frank Norledge; John Hills; Phil Norledge; Bobby Whitby; Peter Hills; Tony Jupp; Tony Merchant; Ernie Halestrap; Charlie Kidd; John Jupp; Redbond; Perry; and Ken Kind

in the days before electric pumps and the wind for the organ bellows had to be supplied manually.

The three Hills children: John, Joan, and Peter (c.1924)

The mention of my curls reminds me of an incident at the beginning of my school days. I went to the Infants' School in St Mary's Lane. This was a wooden building with three class-rooms opening onto a veranda. Miss Jackman, the headmistress, taught one class, Miss Fitzgerald the second, and Miss Caldecourt the third. In fact, Miss Fitzgerald taught the "babies" and I remember being stood on a table on my first day at school to be introduced to the class and feeling very conspicuous. Unfortunately, one of the first things that happened to me was that I got a dirty head, which resulted in the loss of my long hair. Auntie Mary came up to the school and asked to see the children that I sat next to. Miss Jackman said "You know the trouble, Mrs Hills, they will try one another's hats on". I wasn't sorry to lose my curls, because there was a scene every morning when I had my hair done, and I wanted to do the same service for other people. (Auntie Mary had her long hair cut even before she married my father; we three children would stand behind her, take the hairpins out of her bun, and let her plait fall down her back). I thought I would relieve nanny Hammond of her bun. One day, sitting behind her in the deep wicker armchair, I took her hairpins out and was about to cut her hair. Luckily someone stopped me — I did not realise until years later that the old lady had worn her hair on the top of her head to cover a bald patch!

So many Upminster names from the past come back to me. I well remember Searson's shoe shop in Station Road — I think it's likely that my very first pair of shoes came from there. In fact, I know most of the old traders in Station Road. The Jupps, of course, were in St Laurence choir. There was Dad (Len), grandfather ("Old Man Jupp"), Vi (Len's sister) and three of the boys, all with fair hair. A name I hadn't thought of in years was Hubert Cardnell (of Gates and Son, Estate Agents) and "Tiny" Gates, one of my father's friends in the choir.

The forge at Corbets Tey

Dad also used to tell the tale of when grandad went to work and told Henry Joslin that his wife had presented him with the long-awaited daughter, my aunt Helen. The old Essex saying is that a man has not proved himself a man until he has begotten a daughter, and Henry Joslin's reply was "Ha-ha-ha, Jack, you're a man at last!" I gather grandad was not very flattered!

By a quirk of genetics I am almost my mother's double, except that I am about two inches taller than she was. As well as looking like her, I also talked and sang like her. I used to sing when I was on my own upstairs and my father said one day to my stepmother "I wish she wouldn't do that; if I can hear her and not see her, it could be her mother". On one occasion he asked Auntie Mary to ask me not to part my hair in the middle, as it made me look too much like mother. It must have been odd for him, living with one wife and the ghost of another.

I know that my likeness to my mother is true because of two occasions when I was recognised by people who knew her. I had never met my mother's friend, Becky Leach, daughter of the blacksmith at Corbets Tey who had moved to High Easter. My father had sent her a card every Christmas but it was only after his death in 1963 that I paid her a visit, after I saw the name High Easter on a signpost when I was on the way home from a cycling holiday in East Anglia. The people at the Post Office directed me to her cottage across the road and a rather stout little lady opened the door and I said "Hello, "Auntie Becky". She gazed at me for a moment and said "You must be Edie Knight's daughter": she had not seen me since I was a baby at my mother's funeral so I think that first of all her recognition of me came from my voice, and then from my looks.

A few years ago two more people from the old St Laurence choir recognised me. We had all been at Uncle Bert Thorogood's funeral at Hornchurch church and were waiting at the bus stop opposite. A lady and gentleman in front of me turned round, looked at me and spoke to each other. Finally the lady said: "I hope you don't mind me asking, but was your mother Edie Knight?" When I said I was she replied "She'll never be dead while you're alive." I almost frightened Nanny Hammond to death one day. I looked at her round the kitchen door so that she only saw my eyes. I saw Nan go pale and she finally said "Don't you ever do that to me again: I thought it was your mother."

Although I moved from Upminster in 1929 when I was seven, and I have lived away from the local area since 1965, I always feel that Upminster is where I belong: I guess it shows the importance of one's roots. I have named my last two houses *Tadlows* and, having moved over a year ago, I have finally got round to organising someone to put the name-plate up for me!

Isle of Wight April 2000

Open all hours:

Bassett's tobacconists and confectioners

Peter Bassett, with Margaret Ecclestone (née Bassett)

In *Upminster: the story of a garden suburb* (Tony Benton, with Albert Parish, 1996) there is a brief reference to Jack Bassett, who was my father. His full name was John Leslie Bassett and, as the book says, he acquired the lease of a half-shop at 40 Station Road in the mid-1930s where he opened a tobacconists and confectioners shop. I believe that he actually came to Upminster from Wanstead in 1937, when he was 32 years old, bringing his wife Eileen and three existing children, Philip (b. 1931), myself (Peter b. 1933) and Sylvia (b. 1936). He must have opened another tobacconists and confectioners shop almost immediately at the southern end of the Corbets Tey Road parade. John Bassett is listed in the 1937 Trade Directory, suggesting that he had taken over the shop before then.

At the time of his marriage in 1930, our father, then aged 25, ran a cafeteria and tobacconist/confectioners business at 125 High Street, Wanstead. Our parents lived behind the shop, and Philip and I were both born there. The expanded family moved to Spratt Hall

J L Bassett's shop at 40 Station Road, Upminster

Road, Wanstead in 1935 and Sylvia was added to the family in 1936. No doubt tempted by a better lifestyle and an improvement in business prospects in the rapidly expanding suburb, our parents decided to move to Upminster in 1937.

Every Saturday morning before the war Dad, who had an early thirties Morris 10, dropped Philip and me off at the Bell Corner, from where we went off to Saturday morning pictures at the Capitol Cinema in St Mary's Lane, the ticket costing three pence. On your birthday you went free and could take a friend!

Until war broke out our family lived in a rented house, 28 Melstock Avenue, then after a brief evacuation to Blackmore and Hutton, further out in Essex, 69 Park Drive was rented where a fourth child, Margaret was born in July 1941. When war was declared, our father was not conscripted due to medical grounds but instead served in the Police Special Constabulary for five years. His most notable arrest was of a Home Guard officer who arrived at the Huntsman and Hounds public house at Corbets Tey one Sunday morning by car, which ranked as misuse of petrol! Dad also acquired the occasional souvenir, the most memorable being an unexploded incendiary bomb which stood on a shelf in the front room for years.

Father once said that the war brought an unexpected benefit to shopkeepers such as himself, who had been used to extended opening hours. Up until the war his shops were opened every day of the year, including Sundays, except that they closed all day on Boxing Day. But with the war, sweets became rationed and cigarettes were in short supply, so there was no need to keep the shop open for such long hours.

The family doctor, Dr Hendry, was a very relaxed, friendly man who practised in partnership with his wife from their house on the corner of Little Gaynes Lane and Corbets Tey Road. This was handy for us, since we seemed to keep him fairly busy. He delivered Margaret in the "upstairs front" and our ailments included scarlet fever, glandular fever, mumps, two cases of mastoids and one of sleeping sickness.

Along with my brother Philip and sister Sylvia I went to the Bell School. Mr Cox, who had been appointed the first head in 1928 after serving as Headmaster of the old Boys' School, was still head of the junior school in the late thirties. When the school opened in 1928 classes consisted of 50 pupils and there were still 50 pupils in the class when I took the 11 plus exam in 1944. Philip and I both got County scholarships to Brentwood School and went there as boarders in the 1940s, our father having been there in 1919-21. I became a day boy for my last two terms in 1949, using the school bus which departed from a side-road near Roomes Stores. The bus also carried girls to Brentwood County High for Girls, the school that Sylvia later attended. Margaret was only aged 9 when we left Upminster and was still then at the Bell School.

There were two methods of gaining entry to Brentwood School, apart from paying the fees: one had either to pass the 11-plus exam or obtain a Foundation Scholarship. Strangely, Foundation Scholars were not allowed to travel on the school bus which went direct to Brentwood via Warley. Instead they had to make the long journey by train, via Romford.

Eileen Bassett and her four children (Peter, Sylvia, Philip and Margaret) at Clacton, August 1945

Memories of the Bell School in St Mary's Lane, though vague, are not marred by any unpleasant events. Philip and I cycled there as soon as we had two-wheeled bikes and always returned home for lunch. The less-fortunate and long-distance pupils were served school dinners in a purpose-built canteen on site, while the other nutrition available was one-third of a pint of milk in small bottles during the morning break.

The buildings contained, and possibly still do, an Infants' School for ages five to seven, with Mrs Cox as headmistress, and a Junior School (8-11), headed by Mr Cox (no relation). Organisationally, between the two halves were the transitional "Wooden Buildings", where you spent one year at approximately aged seven. These buildings were located on the eastern side of the Infants' playground and were the original temporary classrooms built in 1927 before the permanent brick structure opened the following year. The school was built as an open centred square and the grass quadrangle in the middle was only used for special occasions such as Empire Day (24 May) when we were encouraged to wear the uniforms of any youth organisations we belonged to, and all sang patriotic songs.

A few of my fellow pupils come to mind. Of the girls Judy Needs and Shirley Nash captured my attention for several years. Among the boys remembered are Alan Forey, who lived near us in Rushmere Avenue, and Brian Rasmussen, both of whom went to Brentwood School – the latter playing First Eleven football and cricket and subsequently qualifying as an actuary. Alan Mortlock was another contemporary, whose mother was one of our teachers at the Bell, which gave him special status. The lasting impression of the Bell school, looking back some 60 years, is that the school was a happy one and pupils reached high academic standards.

The Chase leading to Cranham Church, c.1950

One aspect of growing up in Upminster, which many contemporaries may also recollect, was the freedom to roam. I and most of my friends had bicycles which allowed at least a ten-mile range and I also belonged to a "gang" which explored on foot the fields, woods, ponds and railway line around Cranham Church. The area was much wetter in those days which made it more challenging and the railway was presumably that carrying steam trains to Grays, although I never remember seeing one, nor any kindly gent waving from the carriage. Perhaps we weren't angelic enough?

On these travels, two favourite watering holes existed in the '40s. One was an abandoned clay pit to the east of Cranham which had interesting hillocks and ponds, in which the less fastidious swam during the summer. The other favourite was a gravel pit where workings had ceased, presumably due to the war. This was some one and a half miles south-west of Corbets Tey and must be the area shown on recent maps as Gerpins Lane refuse tip. With a group of boys I cycled out there during a war-time summer to find that on a large flooded area the Home Guard had built a raft with a metal superstructure resembling a small tank, presumably for target practice. Upturned, this made an ideal vessel for a half-dozen of us to journey across, regardless of the fact that the majority had not yet learnt to swim.

As already indicated cycling enlarged one's roaming range and when the war ended in 1945 Brentwood outdoor swimming baths became available. Sadly, these baths were temporarily closed down at least once in the late 1940s when Infantile Paralysis (Poliomyelitis) broke out. It was a ride of about six miles from Upminster, mostly uphill through Warley, but of course the downhill return journey was most welcome! The more daring launched themselves at Great Warley and claimed not to pedal until they reached

Cranham! Naturally, the Southend Arterial Road, now the A127, was considerably less busy then.

Our brother Phil's enthusiasm for cycling and watching cricket took him on a return journey of some 44 miles to Southend in May 1948 to witness Don Bradman's Australian test team playing against Essex. Bradman, at the top of his form, scored 187 in two hours and his team knocked up 721 in a single day. Apparently this performance was not meant to belittle Essex but was deliberately intended to establish a psychological ascendancy over England just before the next test match.

Hall Lane by Upminster Common, early 1950s

Because travel was restricted during the war "Holidays at Home" were initiated which consisted of entertainment in the Recreation Ground for a week or so in the summer. Our parents won the Flitch, in a ceremony at Upminster based on that traditionally held at Dunmow, Essex – the Flitch being a side of bacon awarded to the couple who could prove, with witnesses, conjugal harmony for the previous year and a day. Dad was not a naturally keen gardener but "dug for victory". He had tomatoes against the back fence, rows of potatoes, blackcurrant and gooseberry bushes, and a lovely marrow bed.

My sister Margaret's earliest memories are of being in the cupboard under the stairs during air raids (it was decorated with magazine cut-outs) and the Victory bonfire in Park Drive on VE day. There was the excitement of going to the station to catch a train (steam engine!) to town for Christmas shopping and to the pantomime Peter Pan. The two sisters were both members of the Baptist Girls' Brigade in Springfield Gardens, and went to Sunday School there on Sunday afternoons. Afterwards, they walked to the Recreation

Ground to join their parents watching cricket (dad was a keen Essex County Cricket Club fan). The "Rec" had an area with swings, slide and a roundabout, and was a favourite place to play. But one day Margaret came down the slide too fast and still has the scars on her knuckles to prove it (no child-friendly surfaces then!).

Myself, Sylvia and Margaret all had piano lessons from a Mrs Macey in Fairfield Avenue, in Margaret's case starting at the age of four banging a drum. Sylvia and Margaret also had ballet lessons in a bungalow at the top of Park Drive, opposite Dr Hendry, and furthermore Margaret had a few elocution lessons. How feminine girls were then!

Margaret Bassett (with drum) at Mrs Macey's music school, summer 1945

From 1939 until they died in 1957 our maternal grandparents Clara and John Flower lived in a rented bungalow in Acacia Drive. Grandad was the fire-warden for his road throughout the war – that meant that he was in charge of the stirrup-pump. We also had cousins in Priests' Lane, Shenfield and an aunt and uncle with a large house in Meeson's Lane, Grays. The Orsett Show was great fun and we quite often went to Chalkwell or Southend on the train. Zone Restriction applied during the war, which prevented people travelling outside their locality. However, Southend was in the same zone as Upminster so we enjoyed seaside trips without the company of crowds from London as had been the case pre-war. In 1944 the restriction was abolished and that year and the next three we had a summer fortnight at Clacton, with our father joining us for weekends.

St Lawrence Masonic Lodge, Ladies' Night c.1949. From left: Mr Claxton; Eileen Bassett; Mrs Claxton; Pamela Claxton; and Jack Bassett, Grandmaster that year

Our parents were founder members of the Upminster Rotary Club and Inner Wheel. Father was also a member of the Upminster St Laurence Freemasons' Lodge and for a year was Chairman of Upminster Football Supporters Club. Not surprisingly he had many friends among the business community. Percy Scott and Charlie Brech, who ran Upminster

Printing Company at the rear of Dad's Station Road shop, were both called up during the war but were quickly back in business again afterwards. Howard Frizzell owned the bakery business in Station Road – we also knew his wife and daughters. Bert Carter ran the Upminster Club, located behind 65 Station Road, which was licensed and had snooker facilities. Ernie West kept a jewellers shop in St Mary's Lane. Leslie Thomas and his wife Margaret kept a grocers shop opposite my father's Corbets Tey Road shop. While Les was in the RAF during the war, Margaret ran the shop and had to cope with food shortages and the complexities of rationing, coupons, points etc. The greengrocers next door to the Thomases were, quaintly, called S.P.Q.R – Small Profits Quick Returns. Other local personalities were Wylie's the vet, whose children we knew. Also Mrs Peters, who was Welsh and worked as the cashier in Dyer's butcher's shop in Station Road in the 1940s.

I spent a good deal of time in or near the Corbets Tey Road shop. It was en route to school and, being larger than the Station Road premises, had more scope for interesting displays. One of these was specially constructed for the 1937 Coronation of King George VI. The centrepiece was a life-sized chocolate crown seated on a purple velvet cushion. We had the cushion at home for some years but we can't recall who was lucky enough to get the crown. Very soon after the war an early branch of Tesco opened two doors along from our Corbets Tey Road premises. This store definitely operated on the "pile 'em high and sell 'em cheap" policy. The dented and rusty tinned goods can still be clearly recalled!

In 1949 our father acquired the whole of no.40 Station Road, taking over the other half shop which had been Gates Estate Agents. He ran the two shops at either end of Upminster until July 1950 by which time a fall in profits and difficulty getting suitable staff obliged him to sell. The family moved to Battle, Sussex to run a general store and thus concluded thirteen years of successful business life and very enjoyable social activities in Upminster.

Ashtead, Surrey   May 2000

Upminster schooldays

Betty Heath

Our family — my parents William and Annie Heath, my sister Pat, my brothers William (Bill) and Sidney (Sid) and me (Betty) — moved to Upminster in May 1935. In the 1920s my grandfather William John Heath and my father had started a roof slating and tiling business, with the administrative work being carried out in an office in Arthur Street, near London Bridge in London, later moving to an office in Barking Road, East Ham. Thirteen men were employed, one of whom Mr Hopkins, was father's Secretary/Accountant. It was Mr Hopkins who, in the Arthur Street office, taught me how to "draw" 'soldiers' using the keys on the typewriter, which must have been either a Remington, Royal, Underwood or Imperial machine.

This business eventually in the 1930s brought my father into contact with Messrs Alex MacGregor and Alfred Salinger, two builders active in the development of Upminster. Mr MacGregor built for himself and his family (Mrs MacGregor, and their children Duncan

William and Annie Heath, with their children Sidney, Pat, Bill and Betty, early 1930s

and Sheila) a large attractive house on the corner of Parkland Avenue and Corbets Tey Road. The house, which was given the name "Stranraer", was later the surgery of Mr Wylie, the vet. From the names of Mr MacGregor, his children and the house it is more than likely that he had Scottish origins, but as I was quite young at the time so I can't confirm this. He had built a small architecturally attractive office, surrounded by a small garden on the corner of Springfield Gardens and Corbets Tey Road, on the site now occupied from Budgens store to Kurt the hairdresser. Duncan MacGregor eventually joined his father's company in the building industry while Sheila became a nurse. Mr MacGregor's Secretary was Mr Dick Rowe, who lived in Corbets Tey Road with his parents, his brother Gordon and his sister Betty. During the Second World War Dick was, I believe, a pilot in the Royal Air Force. He was captured on operational duty and taken a prisoner-of-war by the Germans, dying whilst still in captivity. My father's company was actively engaged in the development of Upminster in the 1930s and beyond. My brothers joined the company after the Second World War and continued the business until 1992.

We had previously lived in East Ham, which was a pleasant town, not then unduly bustling, with the noise confined to the main road, which I remember had trams running along it. The side roads there were still mostly quiet, interrupted by occasional visits by the barrel organist, playing his lively music, sometimes accompanied by his monkey as a companion and as an added attraction to the performance. Another visiting tradesman was

Parklands Lake, formerly part of Henry Joslin's Gaynes Estate.

the knife and scissor sharpener, who pedalled along on his tricycle, specially adapted to carry his sharpening equipment. On yet another tricycle came the "stop—me—and—buy—one" ice cream man, whose transport was equipped to carry his various items for sale. From France came "The Onion Man", a cyclist with strings of onions over his shoulders. On each visit my mother would buy a string of onions and this same Frenchman came to sell us his onions even when we moved to Upminster.

Whilst living in East Ham we had been fortunate to have many outings to the countryside and to seaside resorts, as a result of which I first knew the Upminster area in 1932 when it was still a village in pleasant countryside. So when we moved to Upminster three years later, we were able to settle readily into the country environment. So it was through my father's business involvement with some of the developers of Upminster that the house we moved into in Upminster was the first to be built in Parkland Avenue, off Corbets Tey Road. With the Parklands lake at the back of our garden our house was named "Park House" by my parents, presumably because of its location. The house - a pleasant four bed roomed detached dwelling with a garage - was built to an individual design by Mr MacGregor, with my father's slating.

Green fields surrounded us and, when the farmer cut the grass, the children were allowed to help construct the haystack with the dried grass. Great fun! Parklands Lake was another source of adventure, in the winter "skating" on the thick ice and in the summer making a raft with planks of thick wood and large tin cans, so that we could float on the water — only one at a time so that we did not sink to the bottom! A large pole was used to push our way from one side of the lake to the other. We were enterprising. There were many trees in our vicinity and tree-climbing became a favourite pastime. We enjoyed walking in the fields and the country lanes which we only had to share with a few cyclists. In the Autumn we gathered the blackberries which were in plentiful supply in the hedgerows, taking the ripened blackberries home to mother. Also in the winter we usually had heavy falls of snow, so we were able to build snowmen and have snowball fights. In the summer we would make a cricket pitch in the field next to the house and muster a team of cricketers, made up mainly of my two brothers, their school friends, and myself. Sometimes a few of my friends would join in too. My position in our team was in the "outback" as a fielder with occasional "treats" as batsman (or batsgirl!). On the same pitch, too, we enjoyed many a game of rounders at which all in the team became expert.

A significant building I clearly remember was Gaynes Manor and its estate. It was there when we first came to Upminster and I can't recall when it was demolished. The mansion was not occupied all the time I knew it, and the various pathways made the estate accessible to us. As far as I can say Gaynes Mansion did not "disappear" until after hostilities had ceased in the Second World War.

Another memory is of Hoppey Hall in Corbets Tey Road where garden parties were held in the summer months. A garage and the Royal Mail sorting office now occupy the site. We had the Recreation Ground in Corbets Tey Road and opposite this were the cottages with their long front gardens - shops now take the place of these.

Advertisement for W J Heath & Son's slating and tiling business from the brochure for the Cranston Park Estate, early 1930s

Entertainment was to be had by visits to the Capitol Cinema in St Mary's Lane, where a supermarket now is. The cinema showed a main and second feature film, a news-reel and a cartoon. During the interval audiences were entertained with lively music provided by a musician playing a Wurlitzer organ. On Saturday mornings only, a special programme was arranged for children, paying an entrance price of tuppence (two old pence - less than one new penny).

Bell Hotel, a few years before its demolition in 1962.

One of the first tasks for my parents on moving to Upminster had been to establish my brothers and I into school. Completion of education in those days for the majority was at the age of 14 years, so by the time we came to Upminster our older sister, Pat, had already finished her education, had left school at the age of 14 and was in employment.

The only mixed school for boys and girls at that time in Upminster was the St Mary's Lane School, which opened in 1927, used by infants, juniors and seniors up to the age of 14. This was frequently referred to as The Bell School, this name presumably originating from The Bell Hotel, which was adjacent to the school. The Bell Hotel was built in 1770 by Sir James Esdaile and Upminster lost one of its most attractive architectural landmarks when it was demolished in 1962.

My father made an appointment with the Headmaster, Mr Frank Cox, to discuss our entry into education at his school and we accompanied my mother and father to meet Mr Cox

Corbets Tey Road, 1949. The cottages have been demolished but part of the site still stands vacant, development interrupted by the war.

at the appointed time. From discussion we learnt that pupils were placed in either "A", "B" or "C" streams in their respective forms. Bill, Sid and I were given appropriate class places.

The next day we attended the school for lessons and I met my teacher, Miss Powell, who came from South Africa. As well as being the Form Mistress, Miss Powell was also the Music Teacher. Other tutors were:

Miss Jackman (Headmistress of the Infants' School)

Miss Berry	Mr Jones	Mr Layrem
Miss Coppin	Mr Frank Lacey	Mr Douglas Westrop
Mr Owen Ellis	Miss Ivy Lacey	

Mr Jones and Miss Berry were married to each other, I think in 1937. Miss Berry probably stopped working after she became Mrs Jones, as in those days ladies were not permitted to continue working outside the home after marriage.

Mr Ellis, who later became the Headmaster of Oglethorpe School, taught arithmetic. I got on quite well with this subject, especially the mental arithmetic, as this was the section I most enjoyed. Mr Lacey was the Art teacher and later became Headmaster of Engayne School and then Deputy Headmaster of Gaynes Senior School.

Bill, Sid and I quickly made many friends. My friends soon included Dorothy Pemberton, Bessie Anglin and Betty Whiting. Dorothy's father was chauffeur to Mrs Williams. The latter was a Justice of the Peace who lived at Upminster Court, which had been built earlier in the century for her late husband Mr A E Williams. Mr Pemberton and family lived in the lodge at the entrance to the Upminster Court estate. Bessie Anglin's parents were the owners of the fresh-fish shop, which was one of the shops opposite Roomes Stores in Station Road. Betty Whiting lived in Argyle Gardens. My younger brother used to accompany me to school from our home in Parkland Avenue and, along the way, we would call for my friend, Florrie Webb, who lived in one of the cottages on the Tadlows estate with her mother and father and her two sisters Elsie and Gladys. All three sisters were born in Upminster and the two older sisters attended the old school in Station Road. Florrie was my special friend, which we have remained to this day.

Further on in Corbets Tey Road we would call for Eileen and Joan Dunlop, and sometimes we would be joined by Stella Cook and Betty Rowe. Early in the morning we followed the school route, walking by cottages opposite the Upminster Recreation Ground with their long front gardens filled with cottage garden flowers. At lunchtime we walked back home (no school dinners in those days - Mother was at home to feed us), back to the Bell School after lunch, then walked home again after we had finished our lessons for the day.

There were two entrances to the school: one on the right-hand side for the girls, the other on the left-hand side used by the boys. Each had to keep strictly to the appropriate entrance only.

Prior to the opening of the Bell School in 1927, the British and the National School buildings were used for the education of boys and girls in Upminster. I remember they continued to be used when I attended the Bell School. I think that Domestic Science for the girls was taught by Miss Wackett in the British School in Station Road. Next to the British School was Abraham's, the bakers, where we used to watch bread and cakes being made and baked in large coal-fired ovens. Next door to Abraham's was Mr Cant, the cobbler. The boys used the National School, immediately opposite the British School, where they were taught carpentry. These two splendid buildings were demolished, the former British School just before the War and the National School in the 1960s.

A lasting memory is of dancing round the Maypole at the Bell School to celebrate May Day each year, which was danced on the grass quadrangle of the school. There, too, we celebrated Empire Day each year — my brother Sidney recalls the Head Boy always gave the Empire Day speech. Sports Days were always great fun and were held in the large field at the back of the school. Races included: the egg-and-spoon race; the sack race; the relay race; and sprint races. Also the three-legged race and the wheel-barrow race. The three-legged race required two boys or two girls, the right ankle of one being tied to the left ankle of the other participant. From the start to the finishing line the two would run as three legs against their competitors similarly tied together at the ankles. The wheel-barrow race again needed individual teams of two boys or two girls. One had to crouch with their hands on the ground whilst their feet were held by their team-mate who helped push the hands-on-the-ground partner along to the finishing line with the hope of winning against their competitors in similar positions. It was essential not to start laughing during the race otherwise the "wheel-barrow" would collapse before being able to reach the finishing line!

Sidney remembers the school colours were blue and yellow, and the football shirts for boys were designed in squares of blue and yellow. A fellow-pupil named Cyril Smith, who was Essex Champion sprinter in about 1937, took fourth place in the All England Sports Event at that time. Swimming lessons were held at the Mawney Road Swimming Pool in Romford. Also, Stanley Eve, who lived in Waldegrave Gardens, became a cricketer playing for Upminster and the County of Essex.

William Heath's Buick car

Joan Brown — who lived in Cranston Park Avenue with her parents Bert and Kathleen Brown, her brother Leslie and her two sisters Ivy and Thelma — started her education at the Bell School in 1934 and became friends with my brother Sidney. They moved to Gaynes Senior School and then to their respective careers, still remaining friends. They married in August 1953 at St Laurence Church and this year they celebrate their 47th wedding anniversary. My friend Florrie married Eric Bacon, who lived nearby in one of the cottages on the Tadlows Estate with his parents and brother Leonard. Eric and Leonard were both born in Upminster where they attended the Bell School.

Upminster at that time was quiet and tranquil. My father did have a Buick car but generally there were very few combustion engines about. Transport was either by railway from Upminster station, which had been built in the 1880s, by the single-decker bus which ran to and from the station from the "The Huntsman and Hounds" public house in Corbets Tey, by cycling or by walking. Mr Brazier, who was also the proprietor of the White Hart in Hacton Lane, drove the bus when the public house was not open for business. On wet days we were allowed to use the bus to get to the Bell School, otherwise we walked to and from school four times a day. One other vehicle I remember bumping along our unmade road in Parkland Avenue was the van belonging to Mr J W Pigg, the baker who served our family with bread and cakes. The junction where Mr Pigg had his bakery at Socketts Heath, Little Thurrock, near Grays became known as Pigg's Corner; Mr Pigg also had a baker's shop in Orsett.

We were fortunate to have a telephone at Parkland Avenue and our number was Upminster 704. In those days telephone numbers had to be obtained through the operator at the telephone exchange in St Mary's Lane (the building still exists near to Somerfield's Supermarket), who connected the caller with the required number. On many occasions we received calls for Roomes Stores by mistake which seems to have been because their number was 740 (although I recently noticed from Mr MacGregor's brochure for the Cranston Park Estate that at that time Roomes' number was 227).

Class 3A Gaynes School 1936. Betty Heath is seated in the second row from the front, fifth from the right.

In September 1936 the brand new school of Gaynes, with Mr Sidney Young as its first Headmaster, opened just for seniors from the ages of 11 to 14. Along with some of my fellow pupils I transferred to the new school from The Bell school, which thereafter no longer took seniors. Among them was my special friend Florrie Webb, while other colleagues were Bess Anglin, Dorothy Pemberton, Vera Watkins and Betty Whiting. Colin Coe, Geoffrey Wallis and Norman Pound were also in our class. My older brother Bill also started at Gaynes on that first day, while my younger brother Sid was to follow in 1938.

On that memorable first day at Gaynes we were allocated to our class-rooms. I found I was in the room on the ground floor of the two-storey building immediately opposite the school hall. I see from my school report that I was in Form 3A and there were 29 scholars in the class, our teacher being Mr F G Lacey, who had been at the Bell School.
Our lessons were:

Reading	Arithmetic (Mental)	Needlework
Language (written)	Arithmetic (Written)	Science
Language (Spoken)	Hygiene	Domestic Science
Spelling	Geography	Physical Training
Literature	History	Games
Handwriting	Art	Music
Composition	Handwork	

All the subjects in the curriculum were taught within the school building and for each different subject we changed to the appropriate class-rooms, up and down stairs and up and down corridors: this was a new experience for us. For swimming lessons we walked to Corbets Tey Road to catch a bus to Mawney Road Swimming Baths in Romford.

I enjoyed being in Mr Lacey's class. He was an excellent artist. I was not, although I always found his lessons were interesting. Other lessons I liked were Mr Westrop's geography and arithmetic, especially the mental sort (I found he made these subjects clear). I also liked music. We played no instruments at school, we just learned the theory, but I was fortunate enough to have private piano lessons which enabled me to achieve the 101 Finger Exercises and the arpeggios! I didn't know too much about science and never got on well with that subject. I made up for that when I later worked in the scientific industry for 27 years. I seemed to get on with the spelling and composition taught by Miss Eidsman. I enjoyed the needlework lessons given by Miss Curzon and I can still remember the "run and fell" seams, the hemming, the back-stitching and the golliwog I made with red trousers and an emerald green coat. Miss Curzon was also the tutor who taught the subject of hygiene. This tuition was given only to girls. Handwork was always interesting, weaving, embroidery and so on, made enjoyable by Miss Grinter.

Games for the girls meant netball. Our pitch was marked out on the girls' side of the playground. I think it must have been football and cricket for the boys. Plus the swimming lessons in Romford. We enjoyed these very much.

A new innovation for us was to have an Open Day, when parents were invited to come

Gaynes School, soon after its opening in 1936.

along to the school to view our work and also to discuss our progress with the teachers. We were allowed to walk around with our parents and receive the "bricks" and the "bouquets" alike.

One of the most exciting events at Gaynes was Sports Day. The competitive spirit was keen and points were awarded to the winners, to be added to the score for their particular "House". I can remember winning my heats and final of the egg-and-spoon race, just luck, I think, that I was able to balance the egg-shaped, egg-sized piece of china on a small spoon and run with it at the same time to a specific point! If the "egg" fell off the spoon we had to start back at the beginning again. I could not remember which house I was representing: was it Deyncourt or Engayne or Esdaile or maybe Latham? My brother Sidney now tells me that, along with our brother Bill, I was in Deyncourt House (Green) whilst he and Joan were both in Esdaile House (Yellow). The house colour for Engayne was Blue and for Latham, Red.

Just as I had at the Bell School, I called for my friend Florrie on the way to school. Gaynes was much nearer to us and, from her home near Tadlows, we were able to continue walking along the path which leads to the side entrance to the school.

School holidays were one week each at Easter, Whitsun and Christmas, with four weeks in the summer during August. An experience I well remember was a holiday with the school to East Cowes in the Isle of Wight. My brother Bill also came and quite a number of pupils went, with several of the teachers. We were accommodated in wooden huts on a campsite with a large playing area. This holiday is now a cherished memory.

Another experience I well recall was the Gaynes Headmaster, Mr Sidney Young, coming into the class-room one afternoon to speak with the teacher (Mr Lacey) who in turn told the class that it had been announced that King Edward VIII had abdicated and this seemed to be a matter of grave concern. The date was Thursday 10 December 1936. The next day, Friday 11th, we heard the King's Abdication Speech, broadcast to the nation on the wireless. The Duke and Duchess of York became our next King and Queen and for the Coronation of King George VI on Wednesday 12 May 1937 each pupil at Gaynes School was given a commemorative book. We were also given twelve penny tickets, a total of one shilling, which we could spend in any of the shops in Upminster. I spent eleven tickets and kept one as a souvenir! We had a day of celebrations in the Recreation Ground in Upminster and the highlight of the activities was a Fancy Dress Parade. Entries, which had to be sent to Miss Jackman at the Infants School, could be made in various sections - boys'

The Cosy Corner café, early 1950s

or girls' fancy dress (entry 1*d*) or decorated vehicles of all kinds (entry 6*d*). There were separate age classes for the fancy dress competition: up to 5 years, ages 5 to 7, from 7 to 11, 11 to 15, 15 to 18 and adult, with ages of young people reckoned as on Coronation Day. Each entry class offered three prizes to a total value of £20 in the form of vouchers, exchangeable at any shop in Upminster, with the biggest and best prizes - 10*s*, 7*s* 6*d* and 5*s* - for the adult fancy dress, the decorated ladies and gentlemen's bicycles or perambulators, or motor vehicles (which were to be stationed along Corbets Tey Road outside the Recreation Ground).

Another memory is of seeing the red-coated huntsmen astride their horses, surrounded by their hounds, on occasions when they gathered outside the "Huntsman and Hounds" public house, ready for their country pursuit. Roomes Stores was then (and still is today) a central point in Upminster. So too was the Cosy Corner cafe, immediately opposite the Bell Hotel on the corner of St Mary's Lane and Station Road, where we enjoyed our tea and cakes and/or ice cream.

At the age of 14 all students had to leave school and take up employment in industry or commerce. I took home my last School Report from Gaynes with my Leaver's Certificate. Because Mr Lacey had given me a favourable write-up my father decided that I should take up my employment in an office. We had no choice of careers: we just had to do what our parents thought best for us. No commercial subjects were taught in schools in those days, so my father sent me to Pitman's College and paid a substantial sum for me to have commerce and business tuition for one year. Then, at the end of 1938, I started work in a London office as a junior shorthand typist at a salary of £65 per year.

On looking back, I recall my memories of Gaynes with affection and remember the Headmaster and teachers as being very helpful and friendly, but with firm discipline throughout the school. My last memory of Gaynes was at the first-ever Old Students' Association function. It was a very pleasant social evening and we were able to meet again the teachers who had worked so hard to establish the beginnings of excellence which was to be the pattern for Gaynes School, also to renew acquaintances with our school friends. The last I remember of the evening was dancing, the ballroom variety, with Colin Coe, who had been one of my class colleagues, before I had to hurry away to be home not later than 10 p.m. Like many, I was not allowed to be out after that time on any evening!

Dances were held at the Bell Hotel to music provided by a live big band. These ballroom dances included the modern waltz, the quick-step, the fox-trot, the old-time waltz, the tango and many novelty dances. Among these were: the Paul Jones, the Valeter, the Lambeth Walk, Under the Spreading Chestnut Tree, the Hokey Cokey and Boops-a-Daisy.

When war was declared on 3 September 1939 we were confronted with gas masks, blackouts, air-raids and rationing of food and clothing, amongst other restrictions. Ration books were renewed annually for use in the next year, a practice which continued until 1954.

The Gaynes' Old Students' Association had to be discontinued on the outbreak of war. In that war, my dancing partner Colin, served as a Wireless Operator/Air Gunner with the Royal Air Force on No. 114 Squadron. He was killed at the age of 21 by enemy action whilst flying on operational duty over Italy on 16 December 1943. Colin is buried in Ancona, Italy, together with the other three members of the crew of their Boston aircraft.

In Upminster during the war we were all occupied in efforts to help win the conflict. Austerity was increasing, small pleasures welcomed and our spare time was used to "dig for victory", which meant growing our own fruit and vegetables, for some being on duty as part of the Home Guard (originally known as the Local Defence Volunteers), for others being on duty as Air Raid Wardens, the ladies joining groups to knit scarves, gloves and balaclava helmets, to be sent to our fighting forces, and many other activities which could prove useful. Besides joining the duty roster as an Air Raid Warden, I became a member of the Knitting Group arranged by Mrs Sandeman, who lived near us in Parkland Avenue. Mrs Sandeman and her husband, who was the Principal of the East Ham Technical College, were both of Scottish descent.

After six years, hostilities came to a winning conclusion for this country, and Upminster then returned to its programme of development.

Upminster. May 2000

Index

INDIVIDUAL AND FAMILY INDEX

Abney, Judy ... 85
Abraham, Sidney, baker & family ... 45, 58
Abraham family, millers ... 9, 44, 87
Aggiss, Lil ... 60
Anglin, Bessie ... 106
Baker, Charles & family ... 41, 42
Bardsley, Miss Frances ... 24
Bassett, John, Eileen & family ... 93-100
Bletsoe, Dr John ... 9, 70, 71
Bolton, Sydney Gladys & family ... 65-74
Bone, Miss ... 20
Branfill family ... 39, 40
Brazier, Frederick ... 54, 108
Brown, Joan ... 107
Butt, Reuben ... 81
Caldecourt family ... 23
Chester, Bob ... 60
Claxson, Walter ... 16
Claxton, Mary ... 86, 87
Cockman, Mr ... 60
Coe, Colin ... 112
Coles, Miss ... 26, 35
Cook, Eliza ... 10, 13, 16, 17
Cooke, Mrs Olga & Miss Lilian ... 66
Copley, Mr ... 33
Cox, Frank J, headteacher ... 56, 94, 105
Cruickshank family ... 85
Curzon, Miss ... 110
Edmunds, Mrs ... 55
Ellis, Owen ... 106
Feltham, Mr ... 54
Gates, Ernest "Tiny" ... 42, 43
German Jinny ... 78
Gillings family ... 27, 33
Halestrap family ... 21-36
Hammond, Bill & Kate ... 76, 84, 85
Hammond, Will & Lucy ... 54, 76
Hayman, Mr ... 54
Heath, William & family ... 101-114
Hendry, Dr ... 94
Hills family ... 51,59, 75-82
Holden, Rev Henry Hyla & family ... 26, 27, 35, 61, 62
Huckle, W ("Bill") ... 24

Ingleton, Jimmy … … … … … … … … … … … … … … …27, 28
Irlam, Alfred … … … … … … … … … … … … … … …54
Ivey, Reg … … … … … … … … … … … … … … … …61
Jackman, Miss headteacher … … … … … … … … …90
Joslin, Henry of Gaynes Park … … … … … … … …22, 56, 90
Jupp family … … … … … … … … … … … … … …26, 58, 90
Knight, Walter John ("Jack") and family … … … … …51-56, 75, 82, 84
Kydd, family … … … … … … … … … … … … … …59, 61
Lacey, F Gordon … … … … … … … … … … … …106, 110
Lambe, Dr … … … … … … … … … … … … … … …52
Lazell, Mrs … … … … … … … … … … … … … …54
Leach, Becky … … … … … … … … … … … … …90
Letch, William & Alice … … … … … … … … … …55, 72
MacGregor, Alex & family … … … … … … … … …101, 102
Moore, Harold … … … … … … … … … … … … …40, 41
Morant, Joe … … … … … … … … … … … … … …54
Nice family … … … … … … … … … … … … … …44, 47
Peters, Sam … … … … … … … … … … … … … …54, 55
Pratt, Cyril & Joe … … … … … … … … … … … …58
Rowe family … … … … … … … … … … … … … …37-39
Sandeman, Mrs … … … … … … … … … … … … …113
Scarff, coachman at New Place … … … … … … …10, 16
Sharp, Herbert & family … … … … … … … … … …7-11
Slocombe family … … … … … … … … … … … …85
Smith, Cyril … … … … … … … … … … … … … …107
Strang, William, (Lord) … … … … … … … … … …54
Sykes, Gerald, Choirmaster … … … … … … … …25, 61, 89
Thompson, "Tiny" … … … … … … … … … … … …47
Thorogood, Herbert ("Bert") … … … … … … … …84, 91
Wakefield, Mrs … … … … … … … … … … … … …23
Warren, Miss … … … … … … … … … … … … … …20
Webb, Florrie … … … … … … … … … … … … …109
West, George … … … … … … … … … … … … …22
Williams, Mrs A E of Upminster Court … … … … …56, 106
Wilson, John & family of New Place … … … … … …7, 11-15
Wilson, Barbara … … … … … … … … … … … … …61
Woolf, Ralph … … … … … … … … … … … … … …22
Young, Sidney, headmaster … … … … … … … … …109

GENERAL INDEX

Coronation, May 1937 … … … … … … … … … … …111
Empire Day (24 May) celebrations … … … … … …56, 95, 106
Flitch ceremony … … … … … … … … … … … … …66, 97
Foden Steam Engine … … … … … … … … … … …44, 54
Football & cricket teams … … … … … … … … … …60
Football team, Boys' School … … … … … … … … …58
Hacton Cricket team … … … … … … … … … … …54
Hockey team, Church … … … … … … … … … … …31
Milk delivery round … … … … … … … … … … …66
Muffin Man … … … … … … … … … … … … … …47

St Laurence Dramatic Society 32, 33
St Laurence Freemasons' Lodge 99
Upminster May Festival & May Queens 26, 27, 35, 36, 48, 67
Upminster Fire Brigade 25

PLACE INDEX
Bell Corner & Hotel 74, 105, 113
Brickworks, Bird Lane 49
Bridge House Inn 47
Bridge Farm 44
Capitol Cinema 94, 103
Chapman's Farm, Hacton 55
Chestnuts Garage 72
Clockhouse, St Mary's Lane 18-20
Corbets Tey, blacksmith 72
Corbets Tey Road 66, 72, 78, 106
Cosy Corner 9, 37, 48, 112
Cranham 96
Deyncourt Gardens 10, 19
Drill Hall, Upminster Hill 47
Eldred's blacksmiths, Bell Corner 19
Garbutt Road 42, 56, 75, 88
Gaynes Lodge 78
Gaynes manor 26, 103
Gerpins Lane gravel pit 96
Hacton hamlet 54-56
Harwood Hall 72, 73
Hoppey Hall 9, 103
Howard Road 60, 65, 68, 73
Hunts Farm, Corbets Tey Road 23, 85
Ivy House, Upminster Hill 37
Malvern, Hall Lane 8, 10
New Place 7-20
Park Corner Farm, Hacton 51-56, 75, 83, 84
Parkland Avenue 103
Parklands Lake 103
Post Office Cottages, Corbets Tey Road 42, 85, 106
Rainham Lodge 54
Recreation Ground/Rectory Fields 60, 98
Rectory Meadows 68
Roomes Stores 68, 109

Schools
- Ardale School, North Stifford 78
- Alleyn Court School, Westcliff 10
- Brentwood School 94
- Gaynes Secondary School 109-113
- Miss Smith's Kindergarten, Ashburnham gardens 10
- Old British School 22, 56, 106
- Old National School 106

- Palmers, Grays … … … … … … … … … … … … … … … … … …59, 66
- Romford County High School for Girls … … … … … … … … …24
- Royal Liberty, Romford … … … … … … … … … … … … … …59
- St Mary's Lane ("The Bell") School … … … … … … … … … …94, 105, 106
- Upminster Boys' School … … … … … … … … … … … … … …22, 56,
- Upminster College, St Mary's Lane … … … … … … … … … …66
- Upminster High School, Hall Lane … … … … … … … … … …8
- Upminster Infants' & Girls' School … … … … … … … … … …22, 56, 82, 90, 95
- Welsh Girls' School, Ashford … … … … … … … … … … … …11
- Woode's, Emerson Park … … … … … … … … … … … … …44
St Chad's Mission Church, Hacton … … … … … … … … … …55, 56
St Laurence Church … … … … … … … … … … … … … … …25, 37, 86
 - Choir … … … … … … … … … … … … … … … … … …25, 61, 88, 89
 - Scouts … … … … … … … … … … … … … … … … … …25
- Sunday school … … … … … … … … … … … … … … …88
St Lawrence Road … … … … … … … … … … … … … … …21, 41
St Mary's Lane … … … … … … … … … … … … … … … …65
Station Road, traders … … … … … … … … … … … … … …8, 70, 71, 90, 99
 - Abrahams Bakers … … … … … … … … … … … … … …23, 56, 58, 72
 - Bassett tobacconists … … … … … … … … … … … … …93-100
 - Battsons diary … … … … … … … … … … … … … … …8, 66
 - Bonanza … … … … … … … … … … … … … … … …59, 65-69
 - Dales newsagents … … … … … … … … … … … … …58
 - Hilberry Chaplin … … … … … … … … … … … … … …68
 - Jupps, butchers … … … … … … … … … … … … … …90
 - Searson's shoes … … … … … … … … … … … … … …90
 - Tollworthy, butchers … … … … … … … … … … … … …70
Tadlows, Corbets Tey Road … … … … … … … … … … … …39, 59, 76-78
Upminster Court … … … … … … … … … … … … … … …66
Upminster Old Chapel … … … … … … … … … … … … …47
Upminster Windmill … … … … … … … … … … … … … …9, 44, 72
Upminster Hall … … … … … … … … … … … … … … …39
White Hart, Hacton … … … … … … … … … … … … … …54

ACKNOWLEDGEMENTS

First and foremost I must thank the authors for agreeing to work with me on recording their memories in this book. I know that they're pleased with their contributions and how they have blossomed from their early beginnings as the months went on and as more of their hidden memories emerged, often in response to my questions. I think it's true to say that at the outset they never thought it would end up like this!

As well as their memories they have also allowed me to use photos from their treasured family albums. The result is a unique and superb series of illustrations that have enhanced the finished articles and added a further personal dimension to this record of Upminster's history. The credit for each illustration in this book is noted below.

I would like to thank my daughter Sarah for acting as my copy-editor and for her useful suggestions, which I usually followed. She also helped with the back cover text. My wife Kay has (as always) supported me on this project over the past year and a half, as I toiled away at my word processor bringing it to this conclusion.

This book would not have appeared when it did without the support and backing of Jeremy Scott at Swan Books who agreed to take it forward through to publication.

It may be that this volume spurs others to put pen to paper. If so, please get in touch with me at 46 Waldegrave Gardens, Upminster RM14 1 UX.

Photo credits: (numbers refer to pages).
Peter Bassett: 93, 95, 98, and 99; Hilda Halestrap: 21, 22, 23, 25, 26, 28, 29, 30, 31, 33, 34, 35, 46 (top) and 88/89; Betty Heath: 101, 104, and 108; Joan and Peter Hills: 51, 55, 57 (top), 61, 62, 63, 75, 80, 81, 82, 83, 84, 87 and 90; Brian Moore: 38 (bottom), 42 and 43; June Muncey: 65, 67 (bottom), 69, and 70; Muriel Sharp: 7, 11, 12 (top and bottom), 13, 15, and 16; Swan Books: 105, 106 and Back Cover; Gaynes School: 109 and 111; Danny Morris: 77; Editor's collection: Front cover, 8, 9, 18, 19, 24, 38 (top), 40, 41, 45, 46 (bottom), 48, 49, 53, 57 (bottom), 58, 60, 67 (top), 71 (both), 73, 74, 78, 79, 85, 86, 91, 96, 97, 102 and 112.

Other local history books published by Swan Books:

Hitler V Havering, by Peter Watt, paperback £11.99.
A detailed account of life in the borough during the Second World War. The book is illustrated with maps, photographs and aerial reconnaissance pictures taken by the Luftwaffe at the time.

Our Old Romford and District, by E.G. 'Ted' Ballard, hardback, £9.95.
This book is about Romford and the surrounding districts of Hornchurch, Upminster, Cranham, Corbets Tey and North Ockendon as it was during the first half of the 20th Century.

The above books are available from our shops in Upminster and Billericay. You can also purchase them by mail-order or via our web site.

We also stock a wide range of local history books from other publishers covering London's East End, Essex and many places further afield!

27 Corbets Tey Road,   57-59 High Street,
Upminster,   Billericay,
Essex,   Essex,
RM14 2AR.   CM12 9AX.
Tel: 01708 222930   Tel: 01277 650686
Fax: 01708 640378
Email: upminster@swanbooks.co.uk   Email: billericay@swanbooks.co.uk

www.swanbooks.co.uk